Catholicism and the
American Mind

Catholicism and the American Mind

by
WINFRED ERNEST GARRISON

WILLETT, CLARK & COLBY
440 SOUTH DEARBORN STREET, CHICAGO
1928

PRINTINGS
First Printing—June, 1928
Second Printing—June, 1928

CONTENTS

Catholicism
and the American Mind

I

THE MYSTERIOUS STRANGER

"Lumpity—skumpka! Lumpity—skumpka!"—intoned in the childish treble of an admired playmate whose eight years imposed authority upon my six, and who marched up and down the back-yard holding an empty flower-pot before him in both hands at the level of his head.

"That's the way the Cat'lics do in their churches. I heard them my own self."

That was, I believe, my first introduction to the Roman Catholic religion. I have since learned that it was inadequate, not to say misleading. But it served me for several years, without substantial addition or correction, as a symbol for the weird ceremonial which that strange tribe called Catholics practiced in lieu of the sensible plain-English Scripture-readings and sermons, the impromptu prayers and the tuneful hymns which constituted the religious *mores* of my own group and therefore of all intelligent people. What it meant to me was that these fantastic imbeciles indulged in a

form of worship that was sheer gibberish, one step
lower in dignity than "eeny-meeny-miny-mo"—a
formula which, however lacking in intelligibility, lent
itself to certain useful applications. One could "count
out" with these cryptic syllables and thus settle doubts
and controversies not otherwise susceptible of adjudi-
cation. But what could anybody do with "lumpity-
skumpka"? And especially in church! It was even
worse than might have been expected from the mental-
ity of the "hired girls" who, as far as I knew, were
the only persons who ever went to a Catholic church.

It was, perhaps, a dozen years later that, as a college
student, I attended a Sunday evening service in the old
United Church on the New Haven Green, and heard
Professor Robinson, one of the most distinguished
members of the faculty of the Yale Law School, ex-
pound and defend the Catholic point of view. I have
forgotten what he said but not my amazement at hearing him say it. My first supposition was that he had
kindly consented to serve as an *advocatus diaboli* to set
up the arguments which the Congregational speaker
who followed was to knock down; or that he was like
an attorney appointed by the court to say what little
could be said for a defendant who could not afford a
lawyer of his own and really had no case anyway. My
surprise was great at learning that Professor Robinson
was not only a Catholic himself but had become one
after reaching the age which is supposed to be that of
discretion. There might, after all, be something in this

matter that would bear looking into. But it was long before I did it.

A great many Americans have never looked into it. To most American Protestants, the Catholic remains a mysterious stranger in their midst, to be viewed with vague suspicion, or with a mingling of condescension and apprehension, or with a good-natured assumption that he must be all right at heart because of the liberalizing effect which America must have had upon the Catholic church.

Their ideas of Catholicism are compounded of an inherited prejudice and a number of vague impressions: a sense of ignorant masses and a domineering hierarchy, mostly foreign and of doubtful morals; a rumor of unintelligible things said or sung, tunelessly, in an unintelligible tongue; mysterious women in black, contrasting with brilliant flashes of color seen occasionally through a church door or in a cardinal's procession or at a eucharistic congress; people telling everything to their priests; priests telling the people how they must act, think, vote; crosses on churches—everywhere crosses, stations of the cross, crucifixes, ghastly bleeding Christs and blue-robed benignant Marys; saints that can be wheedled into doing all sorts of personal favors for those who make the required genuflexions to their relics—knuckle-bones or locks of hair; above all, the pope, a man who claims to be God for all practical purposes but most of whose predecessors in office have been bad examples for the young.

There is some element of fact to account for, if not to justify, every item in this confused picture. The purpose of this book is to clarify the picture, to eliminate the caricature, and to paint in some other features which are worth considering though they do not so inevitably leap to meet the alien eye.

CUT OUT THE CARICATURE

There are good reasons why Protestants and other non-Catholics should try to understand Catholicism. To begin with, Catholics are very numerous and they are not becoming any less so, however firmly some may believe that their system is doomed because of its incompatibility with "modern thought." There are about twenty million Catholics in the United States. How many of them are "good Catholics," no one can say. Neither can anyone say how many of the thirty million Protestants are good Protestants. So that factor may be dropped out of the account. In all matters in which influence is associated with mass activity, the Catholics are probably more influential than the Protestants; partly because they are united in a single body, and partly because they have a more authoritative leadership.

They are not only numerous, but they are intermingled with the rest of the population in social, cultural and political life. We are members of the same clubs, chambers of commerce, corporations, and political parties. We read the same newspapers, support many of the same charities, are victimized indiscriminately by the same enemies of society. We sit beside each other at the opera and the baseball game. We attend the same colleges. If we do not send our children to the same public schools, at least Catholic and Protestant teachers, in numbers roughly proportional to the respective populations, form the instructional staffs of the public schools. A Protestant child in the public schools of almost any city in America is practically certain to have some Catholic teachers during his course. In some cities he is likely to have few others. The frontier between Catholics and non-Catholics not only runs zigzag through our streets; it runs up and down stairs and along the corridors of our apartment houses. We ought to know more about these neighbors whose names and faces are so familiar but whose thoughts are so strange to us.

And besides being numerous in this country, they are even more numerous in other countries. Most American denominations have their greatest strength here but are represented only by small minority groups elsewhere. Episcopalians, to be sure, will find their co-religionists enjoying even greater prestige in England; Presbyterians are in the majority in Scotland; travelling Lutherans find themselves among their own kind in Germany and Scandinavia. But most other American Protestants visiting abroad find that their religion marks them as foreigners almost as definitely as their accent—or would if they let it be known. But the twenty million American Catholics are only a small fraction of the multiplied millions in the world who own allegiance to the "Holy See." To rest contentedly in ignorance of the attitudes and beliefs of so large a proportion of the total population of the globe, just because it so happens that there are but few of this persuasion among our personal friends or in the membership of our neighborhood club, is a hopelessly provincial, not to say parochial, attitude.

Let it be said here, parenthetically, that in this book "Catholic" refers to the Roman Catholic church. This usage is merely for brevity and implies nothing as to its right to the exclusive use of that term.

Great cultures have grown up simultaneously with the growth of Roman Catholicism and in the same area; whether or not by virtue of its stimulus or in the shelter of its protection, at least partly through the activity and genius of the same men. For a thousand years and more it was building itself into the structure of European thought, art, literature, popular customs, and social organizations. The complex body of civilization which existed at the end of the middle ages was intertwined with the history and institutions of Catholicism, even in respect to those factors for which it was not directly dependent upon the Catholic tradition. This civilization, contrary to a certain amount of popular opinion, was not a mass of rubbish to be cleared away. There was plenty of rubbish in it, to be sure, but it was the rich soil out of which were to spring the ideas and institutions of the modern world.

Catholic history is so enmeshed with the general history of European and American civilization that they can not possibly be separated. Some parts of the record of the church may well be an embarrassment to present-day Catholics. Doubtless we would all have occasion to blush for the manners and morals of some of our ancestors if we knew more about them, and it would be much worse if we had to think of them as constituting an infallible body. But merely picking out for unfriendly exploitation those aspects of its past which now seem most open to criticism, is no help toward the understanding of Catholicism as a whole. Some of those items may have to be mentioned presently, though this is not primarily a book of history. But what I am saying now is that the large place which Catholicism occupies in the total stream of western culture justifies a popular interest in its present manifestations.

The fact that most of our religious art is Catholic, that much of our best religious poetry is Catholic, that some of the world's greatest and most inspiring devotional literature is Catholic, that many of the saints whose holy living still illuminates the Christian way of life, and with whom modern men may be proud if they may claim spiritual kinship, are Catholic—these things demand some acquaintance with the system which produced these elements of our common heritage.

A NOVEL AND MONSTROUS CONFLICT

And then, there is the political question. We may as well look it squarely in the eye. Is Roman Catholicism consistent with American patriotism? What, if any, are the possibilities of conflict between church and state when each asserts its right to absolute control within its own field of action and the two fields overlap? Can any Catholic be more than a "provisional patriot"?

A notable English Catholic, Mr. Hilaire Belloc, who writes books which receive the *imprimatur* and *nihil obstat*, says: "The Catholic church is in its root principle at issue with the civil definition both of freedom and of authority.... No one can know the United States without admitting that when the conflict there shall arise, an equilibrium will not be established or preserved, for the conflict will be novel and will seem monstrous. On the one side you have a plain affirmation that the law is the law and must be obeyed, and indignant surprise on the rejection of what seems so obvious and universal a rule. On the other, you will have, as you have had throughout history, resistance and denial to that rule."

I quote these words not to settle the question, but to show that it exists, and that the issue is not one which is raised only by Protestant "bigots" who are gratuitously injecting the religious issue into politics. And since the issue is always coming up in very concrete form—as, for example, in the candidacy of Catholics for high political office—the only sensible course for non-Catholics is to try, with as little prejudice and as much intelligence as possible, to find out what Catholicism really is and what Catholics actually believe and practice.

It is important, but is not altogether easy, to arrive
at an accurate and adequate understanding of Catholicism. The most obvious course, apparently, would
be to read what the Catholics themselves say about it.
This is, in fact, source material of the utmost importance. But it is not enough. If the question is
raised as to whether Catholics are politically trustworthy, it is not sufficient to take their own testimony
and consider the matter settled when they say, Yes,
we are. If, in view of past intolerant attitudes which
have never been officially repudiated and harsh utterances of popes which never can be repudiated, one
asks whether Catholics would be tolerant of other
religions today if they had the power to be effectively
intolerant, it is not enough to have Catholics declare
unofficially that the church has abandoned the policy
of persecution and now believes in granting every man
freedom to practice and propagate his religion.

Catholic writers are, naturally, apologists for their
own system rather than unbiased students of it. With
the exception of such lay writers as Belloc and Chesterton—who delight in paradox, and find a polemic value
in sharply challenging non-Catholic conceptions—those
whose writings are intended for Protestant consumption are at some pains to select for their exposition
those aspects which are most readily defensible. They
try to make it all seem very easy and natural. Catholics are regular people, just like anybody else. They
obey their country's laws, fight their country's battles,
love their country's institutions, believe in toleration

where the civil constitution guarantees it, acknowledge no power above the state in secular matters, and worship God according to the dictates of conscience.

But this, true as it may be, does not cover the whole ground. The non-Catholic must form his opinion of the Catholic church not by merely accepting what it says about itself when it is trying to make a good impression, but by what it says when it is talking to itself and by what it does when it is defining and defending its position with reference to, for example, the state or modern thought.

The non-Catholic who attempts to reach an understanding of Catholic ideas and practices encounters some difficulties. There is, first of all, a sense of strangeness and mystery to be overcome. Catholic churches look different, sound different, smell different, from those to which Protestants are accustomed. There is a bewildering elaborateness of detail in liturgy and equipment, and a meticulous regard for the minutiae of ritual acts and attitudes. There is a multiplicity of symbols, and one does not at once know how seriously to take the veneration with which they seem to be regarded.

PRINCES OF THE CHURCH

There seem to be some fundamentally different mental attitudes, and these are represented by an unfamiliar terminology. In a conservative Protestant assembly one hears appeals to "the Word of God;" in liberal groups, to "the spirit of Jesus;" in almost

any, to "the priesthood of believers," "the right of
private judgment," and "freedom of conscience."
Liberty and equality are emphasized, and the pattern
and the vocabulary of democracy are in the foreground. These things are basic. Those who use
them do not stop to analyze or defend them, because
they are accepted at face value, like gold coins, by
those to whom they are used. Catholics have quite
a different set of phrases to serve the similar purpose
of appealing to accepted concepts and evoking edifying sentiments: "The Church," in a very different
sense; "the Holy See;" "the Blessed Virgin;" "obedience;" "dogma," with no connotation of distress at
its rigidity.

To one who is not accustomed by training to this
phraseology, it is like travelling in a foreign country
and hearing prices stated in strange units of value—
kronen, or rupees, or yen. One supposes that these
indicate certain values to the natives but does not
know how much.

Among Catholics, and especially in Catholic countries, one is constantly being surprised to find some
matters settled with a phrase which, to Protestants,
would mark the beginning of an argument. A nun
in the hospital in Villeneuve, across the Rhone from
Avignon, grew conversational enough to speak of the
spiritual splendors of six centuries ago in the old papal
town. To the remark that some of the cardinals seem
to have been housed with rather conspicuous luxury,

she replied with a proud smile: "Why not? They were Princes of the Church."

Ponder that a moment as a sample of the use of concepts which have validity for the Catholic but not for the Protestant. I am not even hinting that she was wrong, or that she could not have gone on to translate her single phrase into a convincing argument. The point is that she did not think it necessary to do so. "Princes of the Church" covered the whole ground and settled the question with finality. The church, being what it was, would naturally have princes such as they, and these would naturally be housed with a splendor commensurate with the dignity of the church and their position in it.

Understand again that this is not a criticism, but merely an illustration of the difficulty of really understanding. It is evident that every association of people who talk a good deal to each other about their common interests, and very little to anybody else, develop slogans and phrases to stand for those values upon which they agree among themselves—as Democrats talk about Jefferson, and Republicans about the "grand old party." The more they agree upon them, the less they need to justify them by referring back to any more ultimate value. But trouble starts when two such groups try to understand each other, for each uses terms that mean everything to itself but little or nothing to the other. It is like trying to effect an exchange between dollars and francs when neither party knows what the other's money is worth while each considers his own the absolute standard of value. Just so the Protestant, reading a Catholic book or attending Catholic worship, finds himself mystified by the value apparently set upon ideas and words for which he has no particular regard. And even when he gets the idea, he misses the emotional coloring. This is the real obstacle to understanding, for that requires not only that one should know what the other man thinks but how he feels about what he thinks.

ASHES OF OLD FIRES

A still greater obstacle—and one not unrelated to the preceding—is plain prejudice. "We" have already decided that "they" are all wrong, that they are irrational, superstitious, perhaps dangerous, subjects of a foreign power. Besides, in times past "they" have persecuted "us." Perhaps we conveniently forget that, returning evil for evil, "we" also persecuted "them." (The histories that we studied, having been written by and for our side, did not stress that point.) We think of their laity as an ignorant mass, largely immigrants, and of their clergy and "religious," especially the Jesuits, as possessed of a sinister and semi-satanic cleverness, combined with either a senseless asceticism or a reprehensible laxity of morals—or the latter under cloak of the former. Four centuries of intermittent hostility between Catholicism and Protestantism, ranging in seriousness from the religious wars in France, the burning of Protestants in

England under Mary and of Catholics under Elizabeth, and the intolerance of colonial days, to the spasmodic outcroppings of animosity in our own times, have left the ashes of prejudice even after the fires of persecution have burnt out.

The ashes are so hot that sometimes we wonder whether the fires are really dead, and fear is then added to prejudice. Nothing hinders understanding like prejudice and fear, for they take away the will to understand.

I cannot claim to be immune to prejudice. That would be self-praise, and therefore worthless. But I will state my own biases with as little bias as possible, so that allowance may be made for my personal equation. I was reared a Protestant of Protestants, and am one still. I value liberty above authority, place a low estimate on sacraments, and am suspicious of institutionalism in religion. I have Catholic friends and would gladly have more; have worshipped often in Catholic churches, getting uplift from ceremonies which I do not wholly approve and especially from kneeling side by side with those to whom these ceremonies were as the gate of heaven; have visited Lourdes (appreciatively) and the shrines at Einsiedeln and Guadalupe (less appreciatively); and have spent months at Rome. I declined to pay the price of seeing the pope by kneeling to him; but standing on my own two feet, I have been blessed by a French Catholic bishop, after talking the matter over with him.

From which it may be gathered, I hope, that this

is not designed to be in any sense an anti-Catholic book but rather a contribution to the understanding of Catholicism, made with as little prejudice as possible, with entire sincerity, and on the basis of such information as I can command from both Catholic and non-Catholic sources. I shall undoubtedly express some opinions about Catholicism from which Catholics will dissent, for I think the system is wrong on those points which are its distinguishing characteristics. I do not expect Catholics to agree with all my inferences, evaluations and interpretations. But my chief desire in connection with this book is to make its exposition of Catholic faith and practice so accurate and so fair that a well informed Catholic, reading my statement of what Catholics believe and do, will say: Yes, that is exactly what we believe and do.

II

CATHOLICISM IN OUTLINE

Roman Catholicism is two things. It is a form of faith and worship; and it is a form of government. It is a system of beliefs about God and man and the means of salvation, and a system of worship expressing and nourishing those beliefs; and it is a corporate control over the minds, consciences and moral conduct of its adherents—of all the world, if its hopes could be realized—by a very small self-perpetuating group, in the last analysis by one man. "Moral" is an elastic term and may be made to cover much; but even so, it may seem to limit too closely the fields of conduct which the church attempts to control. Nevertheless, I put it in to avoid giving the impression that the church explicitly claims the right to dominate every phase of conduct. It does not do that. But it does claim the right to determine for itself what phases of conduct it has a right to control; which means that it claims the right to control whatever it has any interest in controlling.

Catholicism as faith and Catholicism as government are distinct but closely related. Its faith furnishes the theory upon which the authority of its government rests, and authority is the key-word of the whole system. How true this is, may be gathered from the words of a recognized and accepted defender of Catholicism:

"By the definition which is the very soul of Catholicism, religion must be, for the Catholic, first, a supreme authority superior to any claims of the state; secondly, a corporate and not an individual thing; thirdly, a thing dependent upon authority and not upon a personal mood; fourthly, a guarantee of individual freedom in all that is not of faith." (Hilaire Belloc, in the Century Magazine, April, 1924.)

The entire program of dogmas to be believed, acts of worship to be performed, and authorities to be obeyed, rests explicity upon a world-view in which supernaturalism is the first and most notable factor. Belief in the supernatural is of course no monopoly of Catholicism. Many other world-views and nearly all religions have it, but few carry it so far or lean upon it so heavily. The more conservative Protestants have a theory of the supernatural that is just as definite, so far as it goes, but they make less use of it. Compared with the teachings of Catholicism, the Protestant fundamentalists might be accused of being almost rationalistic. They believe that the Bible is infallible, but they do not believe that anybody is infallibly guided to tell the world what it means. They believe that miracles were wrought long ago, but not now. Catholic supernaturalism is more thoroughgoing. It furnishes not only the foundation but the entire structure of religion. It fills the whole channel of the church's official life, and overflows in miracles and portents in quite unexpected places.

The unfriendly term for describing an extreme form of supernaturalism is "superstition." But that merely means that the party under criticism has recourse to the supernatural in explaining some things which I explain otherwise and that I think he is foolish to do so. To be superstitious is to make too much use of the supernatural. But how much is too much? It is easy to see that the word "superstitious," being thus a purely relative term as between the critic and the object of his criticism, has little value in the description of a religion.

SUPERNATURALISM

The one idea more essential than any other to the Catholic system of religion is that there are two streams of events running through history: the natural and the supernatural. The universe is inhabited by two kinds of intelligences: human and superhuman. The supernatural—that is, the whole range of personalities, forces and events lying outside of the reach of man's ordinary means of knowledge and control and entirely free from the kind of causation that science knows anything about—is not only a perfectly real world; it is a system of reality which is sharply distinguished from the natural world. Its existence may be known by reason and proved logically by the visible effects which it produces in the natural world, but its processes cannot be traced or accounted for by any methods which are available to science. That is the first thing. Not simply a category of spiritual realities but a world of supernatural facts which cannot be blended with the world which science knows by any sort of naturalistic or humanistic interpretation.

This system of supernatural powers and persons, though absolutely different in kind from the forces and creatures of the natural world, is not remote from it. The supernatural has its physical and human agencies through which it is constantly producing supernatural effects in the natural world. Some of these effects are invisible and spiritual, having to do with the salvation of souls, the conferring of special graces and blessings, the guarding of the minds of chosen persons from the possibility of error in religious teaching, and the granting of authority to exercise discipline. Others are visible and physical, miracles performed either to confirm faith or to reward it.

Whoever does not believe in miracles cannot be a Catholic. A large proportion of Protestants also believe in miracles, but for the most part they ease the strain upon credulity by putting them a long way off and a long while ago. They find it easier to accept the story of an ax-head floating at the command of Elisha than they would to believe that a similar event had occurred yesterday in the next block. Peter healed a cripple, and walked out of prison through doors which an angel opened for him and closed behind him. Paul brought a dead woman back to life, and shook a deadly viper from his hand and forgot about it. But a Protestant home missionary who should bring back reports of similar experiences in Oklahoma would be sent to a psychiatrist for examination. "The age of miracles has passed."

But for a Catholic the age of miracles has not passed. He believes that the kind of things still happen which most Protestants believe used to happen. I make no argument at this point as to which occupies the stronger position or whether both are wrong. Some details will be given later about present-day miracles, real or alleged. The point I am trying to make clear is that Catholicism is an out-and-out, thoroughgoing system of the supernatural and the miraculous. It conceives of Christianity as a body of truth supernaturally revealed, miraculously attested, and protected from corruption by supernatural means, and a body of practice supernaturally commanded, and administered yesterday, today, and forever by men supernaturally endowed with authority for that purpose.

MIRACLES AND PROPHECY

The credentials of Christianity are miracles and prophecy which is itself a kind of miracle. The salvation which Christianity offers is an atonement by the blood of Christ. This is the focal point of the whole program of the supernatural, for it involves a sacrifice of and by a supernatural being and a supernatural process of redemption wrought upon man thereby.

This does not differ in principle from the older Protestant theology. But what follows does differ from it in an important respect. For according to the Catholic theory the Church is a supernatural institution charged with the responsibility of conserving and applying the benefits of this atonement and endowed with supernatural grace and authority to that end.

If I have used the word "supernatural" with tedious iteration, it is to make the idea unmistakably and unforgettably emphatic. Catholicism can have no fellowship with any modernistic or humanistic view which blurs the distinction between the natural and the supernatural, or which views religion as a distillation from human experience, or which thinks of Jesus as merely the "highest expression" of something in human life and of salvation as progressive improvement in the art of wise living under the impact of all good influences, of which Jesus is perhaps the best. The whole system of ecclesiastical authority goes to pieces on any such basis as that.

That is not to say that the Catholic Church maintains its conception of supernaturalism merely to support ecclesiastical authority. No one has a right to impute any such motive. But the whole thing goes together, whichever end one starts at. Catholicism presents a thorough and consistent system of supernaturalism, expressing itself in both physical and spiritual miracles, which begins with creation, and comes down to the present moment, and goes on into the future as supernatural and as miraculous as ever.

At the present time, the supernatural functions which concern men are of three sorts, one of which conservative Protestants admit and two of which most Protestants deny. The one they admit is the redemptive power of Christ and the spiritual blessings which accompany faith, prayer and worship. The two that they deny are the supernatural authority of the church in matters of both faith and discipline, and the continuance of physical miracles.

Or, to state a little more fully the issues between Catholics and Protestants, this thoroughgoing system of supernaturalism, when applied to the church, becomes the support of three major convictions which Catholics hold and Protestants do not:

First, the perfection of the Catholic religion as a system of doctrine and practice. It has been defined with increasing clearness and rigidity through the centuries, in reply to attacks of heretics or to meet other emergencies, but the system itself is supernaturally perfect and is now exactly what it was when it was first revealed by Christ and what it must always be. The Roman church therefore has nothing to learn from any other source. It cannot compromise, confer, or cooperate, where such action would cast any doubt upon its assurance of its own perfection. The latest expression of this is found in the encyclical of Pius XI issued Jan. 6, 1928.

Second, the infallibility of the visible church as the agency to which God has entrusted the preservation, definition, administration, and propagation of that perfect system; and specifically the infallibility of the pope as the head of the church and the personal representative of Christ.

Third, the authority of the church over its own members in all matters which it defines as related to faith and morals, and its inherent right to exercise all the powers and functions, temporal as well as spiritual, which, in its own infallible judgment, are necessary to the discharge of the duties enumerated above.

FROM ADAM TO PIUS XI

There is a continuity of direct supernatural interventions in human affairs from the creation of man to the present time. Much use is made of the analogy between the religion depicted in the Old Testament and Christianity. Supernatural revelation and prophecy began with Adam. The long lives of the antediluvian patriarchs facilitated the faithful oral transmission of the doctrines which had been delivered to Adam. One can easily see what great advantages would be possessed, for the purpose of handing down tradition, by a race of men who lived to be eight or nine hundred years old and whose lives overlapped those of six or eight generations of their descendants.

After Noah, and especially after Abraham, the narrowing of the channel of transmission to a chosen family and race further tended to preserve purity of doctrine. Later, God "established a perpetual body of teachers, called the synagogue, to spread the knowledge of that revelation . . . The synagogue was a figure of the future church of Christ, and it had permanently a high priest, whose office corresponded at many points to that of the pope. Would God have given a more perfect organization to the figure than to the reality?"[1]

Inspired prophets were sent to be the "infallible interpreters" of the revelation. And so, by the succession of patriarch, prophet, priest and synagogue, "the pre-Christian revelation was preserved substantially intact till the coming of the Messias." There was a foreshadowing of the future even in the fact that, while the synagogue leaders became personally unworthy, nevertheless they kept the true doctrine, so that Jesus could say: "All things whatsoever they shall say to you, observe and do, but according to their works, do ye not." Here a basis is laid for the very necessary distinction between impeccability and infallibility. God uses sinful men as the infallible guardians of his revelation. Even popes may be morally wrong in their deeds, but they are infallibly right in their teachings—even about morals.

It is to be observed that the pre-Christian revelation is represented as having been preserved chiefly through an authoritative and infallible organization. Documents were useful but incidental. The chief de-

---

[1] The quotations in this chapter, where not otherwise credited, are from Charles Coppens: "The Systematic Study of the Catholic Religion" (Herder, St. Louis, 1925).

pendence was upon a succession of living men, handing down a tradition by word of mouth, and supernaturally endowed so that they might do so without error.

TRANSMISSION BY AN INSTITUTION

Continuing the method which is alleged to have been that by which the doctrines revealed to Adam, Abraham, and Moses were preserved and transmitted, the Christian revelation also is handed down chiefly through oral, personal and institutional channels, and not primarily by the incorporation of it into documents by reading which anyone can arrive at a knowledge of the truth. The documents are important, to be sure. Something will be said presently of the Catholic attitude to the Bible, and especially the New Testament. It is not what Protestants often suppose it to be. But whatever it may be, the Catholic theory is that the chief dependence is upon other than documentary agencies for the preservation and propagation of the faith. I summarize the argument for this position without criticizing it.

Christ did not write and he did not tell his followers to write. He chose a group of men to receive and transmit his teachings. He taught them and told them to go and teach others. "He evidently had given no sign that he intended the enlightenment of the world to be procured chiefly by written documents." At that time and for centuries after, few could read, and there is no evidence that the apostles or the Christian teachers of the first centuries made any special effort to raise the percentage of literacy or to scatter the written word among the masses. Irenaeus reported that the barbarians "believed in Christ without ink and paper." Religion, in short, "was not designed to be learned from the Scriptures chiefly."

The New Testament record gives some data which enable us to form a picture of the development of the church as the authoritative teaching body entrusted with the keeping and dissemination of the Christian tradition:

The Twelve were the nucleus of the "teaching church."

Peter was designated for a position of special importance. "On this rock I will build my church."

The promise to the Twelve, "Whatsoever you shall bind on earth shall be bound in Heaven," was a direct grant of authority.

The injunction to the Twelve at the Last Supper, "Do this—," gave to them and to those authorized by them the power to perform the miracle of the mass.

The promise that the Holy Spirit should guide them into all truth applied to the apostles and their successors.

The "great commission" was a command and a promise: "Go—preach—baptizing—teaching them to observe all things whatsoever I have commanded you —I am with you even to the end of the world." As the apostles could not live to the end of time, this was not limited to them but applies to the church as a teaching institution of which they were the beginning.

The apostles received miraculous power and went preaching, "the Lord working with them and confirming the word with signs that followed." (Mk. 16:20).

The filling of the vacancy caused by the defection of Judas suggests that a continuing organization was contemplated, with power to fill vacancies.

The Twelve continued to govern and teach the church in Jerusalem.

The apostles appointed others to teach, that is, ordained bishops, directing them in turn to ordain others. Paul's instructions to Timothy about the selection of bishops occur in close connection with the statement that the church is "the pillar and ground of the truth" (1 Tim. 3:15), and this is followed by still more specific directions about the establishment of an oral tradition (2 Tim. 2:2). He gave similar instructions to Titus (Tit. 1:5, 9).

Scarcely had the last of the apostles passed away when Clement of Rome wrote: "The apostles made these appointments and arranged a succession, that when they had fallen asleep other tried men should carry on their ministry" (Epistle to Corinthians, 44). A few years later Irenaeus made apostolic tradition the test of truth: " All that have the will to know the truth may find in every church the Tradition of the Apostles." Less than a century after that, when the process of sifting the literary products of Christianity and collecting some of them into the New Testament was already well advanced, Tertullian refuses to argue with heretics on the basis of Scripture because they misinterpret it, and appeals to the churches founded by the apostles as possessing a true tradition.

Set this down, then, among the important Catholic ideas: that the chief factor in the preservation of the truths of Christianity is institutional, rather than documentary; a succession of persons rather than a collection of texts; in short, ecclesiastical tradition rather than the Bible. We must therefore see a little more fully what Catholics think about the Bible, and what they mean by tradition.

ROMAN CATHOLICS AND THE BIBLE

For Catholics, the Old and New Testaments are truly "the Word of God"—"without the slightest taint of error." Inspiration, as defined by Leo XIII in the encyclical *"Providentissimus Deus,"* in 1893, includes three elements: God "inflamed the will" of the writers so that they were moved to write. He furnished the necessary knowledge of historical facts and religious truths, in some cases by direct revelation, in others by guiding the writers in their search for and choice of material. And he restrained them from including any erroneous statement in their writings. All the statements in the original text are true, and not merely those of doctrinal or moral importance. It is not claimed that the text has been kept uncorrupted by supernatural means.

The contents of the Catholic Bible differ from those of the Protestant Bible chiefly in including certain books which are found in the Greek translation of the Old Testament, known as the Septuagint, but not in the Hebrew texts known to us. These are the books of Judith, Tobias, Ecclesiasticus, Wisdom, Baruch, 1 and 2 Maccabees, and certain additions to the book of Daniel. The reasons for using the Greek rather than the Hebrew canon are that the Greek version was more widely read than the original Hebrew by Jews at the time of Christ, and that it was more frequently quoted by early Christian writers. Origen, in the third century, favored the Greek canon and considered it ridiculous that Christians should "humbly bow to the decisions of the Jews"—even in regard to what books constituted the Jewish Scriptures. (An interesting echo of anti-Semitic sentiment in the early Gentile church, which was still sensitive about its independence of Jerusalem.)

The Council of Carthage in 397 confirmed the Greek canon; Innocent I, in 410, approved it as the Catholic canon; and the Council of Trent re-affirmed it.

The Latin version of the whole Bible, made by Saint Jerome in the fourth century and called the Vulgate, is now considered the authentic and authoritative form of the Scriptures. All translations into modern languages must conform to the text of the Vulgate, which has been revised to incorporate many of the results of textual criticism. They must also contain notes explaining passages which are liable to misunderstanding by the unlearned. The standard English version is the one published partly at Rheims in 1582 and partly at Douay, France, in 1609, revised and annotated by Bishop Challoner in 1750.

These facts should throw some light upon the statements, often heard, that the Catholic church keeps the Bible away from the people, burns Bibles, opposes Bible societies, and so on. They are literally true. The Catholic church has done all of these things—but not because it opposes the teachings of the Bible *as it understands them*. It has burned Protestant Bibles because it claims that they have an incorrect text and are liable to be misunderstood on important points of doctrine. It opposes Bible societies because they circulate Protestant Bibles. It keeps the Bible away from the people in many cases —not always—because it thinks the Bible is a difficult book to understand and that the oral teaching of the priests is a safer method of presenting what it believes to be the truth.

The difference in text between the Catholic and Protestant Bibles is not by itself a matter which could arouse much emotion. It is true that the Catholic Bible contains half a dozen more books, but it is scarcely likely that the average Bible-reading Catholic spends much more time on Esdras and Maccabees than the average Protestant does on Chronicles and Zephaniah. The differences in translation are sometimes significant, as when the Douay version reads "do penance" where the King James version has "repent." The most important thing, however, and the thing that moves the Catholic church to oppose so strongly the circulation of the Protestant Bible is that it lacks the notes and explanations which alone guarantee that the reader will get the "true Catholic sense."

But however much or little the actual differences may be, Catholics take them very seriously. Thus we find it recorded in the Vatican organ, *"L'Osservatore Romano"* (Rome, June 1, 1923): "After the sacred function on Sunday in the Church of S. Maria della Navicella, in the piazza, while the facade of the basilica was illuminated with torches, a characteristic ceremony took place. Many pornographic books, immoral pictures and Protestant Bibles seized from the hands of boys were thrown into the flames in honor of the Madonna."

Early in the nineteenth century there was much excitement in several countries in Europe over the activity of the Protestant Bible societies and the means that were being taken to restrain them. Metternich, the Austrian chancellor, wrote an interesting letter to Nesselrode, the Russian prime minister, dated Aug. 20, 1817, in which he states his own view of the matter. He says:

"The Catholic Church does not encourage the universal reading of the Bible, and in this respect it acts like a father. The Church not only allows but recommends the reading of the sacred books to men who are enlightened, calm, capable of judging the question. She does not encourage the reading of passages full of crimes and obscenities which the Book of Books

contains only too often in histories simple like the
first ages, and like all that is true. For myself, I
think the Church is right, and I judge by the effect
which the reading of the Bible has on me at the age
of forty, so different from that which the same reading produced on me at the age of 15 or 20 . . .
At 20 I tried to understand the Apocalypse; now I am
sure that I shall never understand it. At the age of
20 deep and long continued research in the Holy Books
made me an atheist; now I believe and do not
criticize."

Metternich, to be sure, has no standing as a Catholic theologian, and one need not trust too implicitly
the truth of his statements about the dire results of
the "deep and long continued research" which he conducted in the Scriptures in his boyhood. But his letter represents one angle of the Catholic view as seen
by a layman who was also a politician and a diplomat.
The Bible is not a simple body of edifying religious
teaching, but a complex mass of material, some of
which is too realistic to be edifying for the young and
some of which is easily misinterpreted by the simple.

Luther, very soon after 1517, arrived at the decision that the Bible is perfectly clear; that every
passage has one obvious meaning which anyone can
grasp who will simply read it; that "the Holy Spirit
is the all-simplest writer." The divergent theologies
which claim to find support in it forbid most Protestants today to take quite that extreme view of the
matter. The Catholic Church, on the other hand, holds

that the Bible is sufficiently difficult to interpret so
that heretics may make it teach heresy. The church
must therefore impose the interpretation which is supported by its infallible authority. "No Catholic is at
liberty to put novel interpretations upon the texts
of Scripture not in accord with the true Catholic
sense." The Council of Trent specifically forbids all
interpretations at variance with the unanimous consent of the Fathers when they speak as witnesses of
the tradition of the church.

"Tradition," then, must be immensely important.
What does the Catholic church mean by tradition?

TRADITION

Dismiss from your minds the connotations of un-
certainty, rumor, legend, dubious truth. Tradition
means something handed down. A tradition may be
at variance with the original truth which it professes
to transmit if the channel through which it is transmitted is one that allows the admission of error. Human traditions are inevitably of this sort. Or a tradition may preserve, with or without variations, something which never was the truth. That depends upon
what it is that is handed down. But, so far as the
meaning of the word is concerned, a tradition may be
either true or false.

Human nature being what it is, prone to misunderstanding and inaccuracy, the presumption is against
the oral transmission of anything very long or through
many persons without considerable modification. Try

it by whispering a message around a circle of friends, or by noting how scandal accumulates circumstantial details as it circulates. But this presumption of inaccuracy may be combatted by evidence, either by checking the tradition against an original written record or by proving that the channel of transmission was guarded in some effective way from error. By both of these means Catholics believe that they can substantiate the truth of their tradition.

Catholic tradition means "all the doctrines which Christ and his apostles delivered orally to their disciples and which were not written in the sacred pages. It thus includes the canon itself of the Scriptures and the proper interpretation of all their contents." It also includes much besides, as will presently appear. In the Catholic view, tradition takes precedence over Scripture, not in the sense that it is to be followed when the two conflict—for it is not admitted that the two ever can conflict—but in the sense that Scripture depends upon tradition both to establish its standing as Scripture and to tell what it means. "Augustine said that he would not believe the Scriptures if it were not for the authority of the church; that is, he might accept them as valuable historical documents, but not as the Word of God, if the tradition of the church did not teach that they are such."

Here, then, is a clear-cut difference between the Catholic and Protestant views. The classic Protestant dictum that "the Bible and the Bible alone is the religion of Protestants" is an affirmation that the Bible may be known for what it is by an examination of it and does not require to be validated by the tradition of the church, and that, so far as authority is necessary in religion, the Bible is a sufficient authority since it contains all that is "requisite and necessary to salvation."

Ecclesiastical tradition includes the following kinds of materials: the liturgy and ritual; the history of the church, especially of the early church and of the acts of the martyrs; the testimony of archaeology to events and beliefs in the past; definitions of doctrines, decisions and anathemas, whether pronounced by the pope or declared by general councils and confirmed by the pope; the writings of the Fathers, who, while they may err as individuals, constitute an unquestionable proof of a genuine tradition when they are in agreement; and the writings of certain saints of extraordinary learning, designated as Doctors of the Church, especially Athanasius, Basil, Gregory of Nazianzen, Chrysostom, Ambrose, Augustine, Jerome and Gregory the Great. These, like the other Fathers, do not create tradition by virtue of any special revelation to them individually, but bear witness to an existing tradition. The tradition itself is the teaching of the church—that is, "of the bishops under the headship of the Roman pontiff." These several items that have been enumerated constitute the witness to what that teaching has been and the means by which it has been handed down.

The question as to the authority of tradition, therefore, ultimately becomes a question as to the nature of the church. Something has already been said of that, but a fuller statement must be made.

A CRITICAL PARENTHESIS

Before expounding the Catholic doctrine of the church, it may be said parenthetically that the whole argument, in regard to both the authority of tradition and that of the church appears to me to rest upon a false assumption, namely—that the success of Christianity and the salvation of souls demands the handing down of a doctrine that can be certified as infallibly true. A Catholic writer says: "If the Scriptures had been intended to be the sole guide of faith, the apostles would necessarily have composed a systematic, full, and clear exposition of the faith." This sounds reasonable—if the transmission of a perfect and complete body of doctrine were the object. But one might also say, with equal plausibility, that if the "teaching church," consisting of a perfectly articulated hierarchy headed by the Roman pontiff, had been intended to be the sole guide of faith, the apostles, or Jesus himself, must necessarily have left a systematic, full and clear exposition of the constitution of such a church.

The answer to both of those arguments is that, when the records and the history are critically examined, it does not appear that Jesus considered that the handing down of a body of infallible doctrine, whether through inerrant writings or through an infallible tradition, was a matter of importance. The assumption that it is necessary to have an infallible answer to every doctrinal or practical question that can arise gives great weight to the Catholic claim that the church *must* be infallible because the Scriptures, though also infallible, are not so clear as to decide all points of doctrine. But if that assumption is challenged, the claim crumbles.

THE CHURCH

Assuming, however, the necessity of an infallible teaching and ruling body to preserve the "deposit of the faith," Catholicism finds that Christ established the church as "a permanent institution which would derive its permanence from its relation to Peter." It began its objective existence on Pentecost with the descent of the Holy Spirit and the conversion of three thousand. These became the "assembly," while the Apostles constituted the "teaching church." This distinction is vital and permanent. The great body of members of the church contribute nothing to its authority or infallibility. It is the hierarchy which, inheriting the authority of the apostles, constitutes the succession through which tradition is transmitted and to which such grace is granted that it cannot err in its declarations of truth. It is the hierarchy also, and not the whole church, which exercises the three functions corresponding to Christ's three as "prophet, priest and king"—namely, to teach, to administer sacraments, and to rule. "As Christ is king, the church is a perfect and independent society. She can make laws in spiritual things for all who by baptism have become her subjects; she can judge them, and *coerce the contumacious.*"

This matter of coercing the contumacious sounds rather ominous. The church might go a good way under that charter. In fact, it sometimes has gone to lengths which need a good deal of explaining, or forgetting, in these democratic days. But it must be remembered that the Catholic church is frankly built upon a monarchical, not a democratic, pattern. "In every society there are governors and governed. So in the church. Most Protestant churches regard their officers as merely servants of their constituents, not having authority over them. The Catholic church regards its governors as commissioned and empowered by Christ as successors of the apostles."

There are three essential societies: the family, the state, and the church. Each is complete and independent in its own sphere, but each should foster the other two. And since the Catholic church is the only legitimate church, the state should foster the Catholic church. "When parents grossly and plainly violate their duty, the state can control them. In like manner, the church can curb the gross excesses of the state by solemn condemnation and spiritual punishment." From which it would appear that the relation of the church to the state, as of the state to the family, is one of superior authority in judging when duty is violated. The punishments, however, are "spiritual."

Do Catholics teach that all Protestants are

damned? They do not. Perhaps logically they ought, but actually they do not, any more than immersionists teach that the unimmersed are damned. The Fourth Lateran Council decreed: "Out of the Church no man can be saved." Yet there is such a thing as "invisible communion" with the church. "If it is impossible for a person to join the church, or if he is invincibly ignorant of this duty, he is excused from sin in this matter. So long as he is really unable to remove doubt, so that he cannot see that it would be prudent for him to join the church, he is not to blame."

It has always seemed to me that this "invisible membership" is rather a weak evasion. But if it is a logical error, it is an error on the side of charity. It was Pius IX, staunchest of ultramontanists, who said: "God does not inflict eternal punishment but for wilful sin." To the Catholic mind it seems safer to admit an "invisible membership" in the visible church, than to admit the existence of an invisible church. The one and only church—with its four marks, unity, sanctity, catholicity, and apostolicity—must be conceived of as a completely visible society; otherwise some of that endowment of grace by which it possesses infallibility and exercises authority might be resident in the invisible part of it.

These few basic ideas suggest the points which are most distinctive of the Catholic interpretation of Christianity. No mention has been made of the particular doctrines which make up the Catholic theology, or of the specific acts which constitute the program of worship, or of the details of the ecclesiastical organization which has been created to administer the authority resident in the church. All that can come later, together with some consideration of the situations which arise when a church holding that exalted notion of its own unique power and dignity finds itself in a society most of whose members deny its claims.

But as this chapter began with an emphasis upon the rather abstract idea of the thoroughgoing supernaturalism of the system, it must conclude with a reference to the very concrete fact that the present authority which that supernaturalism implies is summed up and concentrated in the pope.

Catholicism is a religion of centralized authority. Authority to teach and govern resides in the church. But exactly where in the church? Certainly not in the laity, and not in the lower clergy. Leo XIII denounces "that most pernicious doctrine which would make of the laity the factor of progress in the church" and the modernistic heresy that "a share in the ecclesiastical government should be given to the lower ranks of the clergy." Not in any single bishop. • Not in all the bishops together. Not in a general council. "There is but one infallibility, Christ's; and Christ, organically united with the church, communicates to her his infallibility, and with that infallibility the pope is equipped,"—says C. C. Martindale.

We must therefore consider in more detail the idea of infallibility and the twin concept of temporal sovereignty.

III

THE POPE GAINS AND LOSES

Spiritual infallibility and temporal sovereignty are the two principles upon which the papal absolutism rests. The main purpose of this chapter is to explain what Catholics mean when they say that the pope is infallible, and how that became an article of faith; and to tell what the temporal sovereignty of the pope means, how he lost it, why he wants it, and what are his prospects of getting it back.

A Catholic writer would not place these items so near the front of his book, and perhaps he would be right in deferring them, for the church existed many hundreds of years without either—or at least without suspecting that it had the one or dreaming that it would ever possess the other. But if these are not the foundation stones of the Roman Catholic system, one of them is the keystone of its arch, the other the cap-stone of its spire. If the fitness of a candidate for admission to the Catholic church were to be judged by his answer to a single question, undoubtedly that question would be, Do you accept the infallible authority of the pope? It might not be phrased in just that way, but that is what it would mean.

To be precise, the oath which the Catholic convert is required to subscribe is (in part) this: "I believe all the articles the church proposes to my belief, and I reject and condemn all that she rejects and condemns, and I am ready to observe all that she commands me." And the Catholic Encyclopedia says: "The papacy is the crown and center of the entire constitution of the Catholic church. The papacy includes in itself the entire fulness of the power of administration and teaching bestowed by Christ upon his church."

What happened in Europe during the nineteenth century cannot be ignored in considering what is happening in America now. The Roman church is an international corporation, and what it does and what it is anywhere affects it everywhere. So in going back across an ocean and a century for a chapter, we are not for a moment diverging from the inquiry into what it means to be a Catholic in America today.

THE CHURCH FACING DISASTER

In the latter part of the eighteenth century, just at the time when the church was setting up its new household in the United States and preparing to develop under such conditions of absolute religious freedom as it had never enjoyed in any non-Catholic country—and has never permitted Protestantism to enjoy in any Catholic country—Catholicism in Europe seemed to be in rather a desperate condition.

The Jesuit order, which had been the pope's right arm for two hundred years, had fallen into bad repute. Its quarrels with other orders destroyed the peace of the church, and it was so generally suspected of political intrigue and of dangerous teaching in both morals and theology, that it was suppressed by a papal bull in 1773.

The intellectual movement which culminated in that rationalistic philosophy known as the "Enlightenment" meant revolt against the whole system of theological dogma, both Catholic and Protestant. Its most definite antipathy was against the Catholic ideas of ecclesiastical authority and supernaturalism. Men who considered themselves abreast with the free thought of the age had little patience with the wonder-working relics which were the church's most visible stock in trade, or with the methods of violence and intolerance on which it had, to be sure, no monopoly, but of which it was the most expert practitioner. Humanitarian philosophers were preaching tolerance, while Philip V of Spain was burning a thousand heretics during his reign in the interest of Catholic orthodoxy. The "enlightened despots," such as Frederick the Great, who were patrons of literature and philosophy, contrasted favorably with the sort of intellectual tyranny of which the pope appeared to be the most typical representative.

A series of nationalistic movements threatened to lead to the establishment of national churches owning only a nominal allegiance to the papacy. The spirit of independence which had made "Gallicanism" a peril to papal absolutism in France was ready to break out again. The German clergy, even the archbishops, conspired against the papal supremacy. Austria under Joseph II was taking a course much like that of the most extreme Gallicanism. Even in Tuscany similar reforms were voted at the synod of Pistoia under the lead of Leopold, brother of Joseph II. It seemed a reasonable guess that what had happened in England under Henry VIII would happen in half the countries of Europe before the end of the eighteenth century.

Papal diplomacy had lost prestige through backing the losing side in every war of the century. The Bourbons took Naples, in spite of the Pope's claim to overlordship. The War of the Austrian Succession crippled and diminished the States of the Church, and the peace of Aix la Chapelle ignored the Pope's claim to Parma and Piacenza. The representatives of the popes were snubbed at every diplomatic gathering.

The financial difficulties of the papacy were constant and embarrassing. Its struggle with poverty and debt was varied, but scarcely alleviated, by recourse to disreputable means of raising money. We look with scorn upon the strawberry festivals and rummage sales by which indigent churches try to meet their deficits, and say "Rome never does that." But Clement XI debased his own currency. Clement XII established a papal lottery and, by way of protecting home industry, excommunicated patrons of the rival lotteries of Genoa and Naples. Benedict XIV levied a stamp tax which was a failure. Clement XIII raised a forced loan when, during the fight on the Jesuits, France and Naples suspended all payments to Rome.

Pius VI issued fiat money, emitted a bond issue which nobody would buy, thereby precipitating a financial panic, and farmed out the taxes of the papal state, discounting them years in advance. The Vatican was, in fact, tottering precariously on the brink of bankruptcy.

What its friends could not do to save it, its enemies did. The French Revolution and the deluge of disaster which Napoleon poured over Europe frightened all the conservatives and even the semi-conservatives into reaction. If we consider how "bolshevism" has been used as a bogey-man in our own times to rouse fear of social and political liberalism, we can easily understand how useful were the spectres of the reign of terror, the "worship of reason," and the upstart Corsican in frightening the timid back into the conservative fold. The ancient institutions of church and state had seemed on the verge of dissolution and the world was being turned upside down between 1789 and 1815. When Waterloo and the Congress of Vienna brought this bad dream to an end and gave Europe a chance to reconstruct itself, the most obvious thing to do in the interest of safety was to exalt the old institutions—the Roman Catholic church and the monarchies under their "legitimate" sovereigns.

The history of the first half of the nineteenth century in Europe was the story of the struggle between the democratic spirit and this force of reaction. The fortification of the position of the church involved the return of the pope from Fontainebleau to Rome, the re-establishment of the Jesuit order, the re-organization of the Papal State on the most absolutistic lines, the making of new concordats between the Vatican and the various governments, the development of new cults for the encouragement of Catholic piety, and the growth of the movement known as "ultramontanism" which involved a more thorough concentration of all authority at Rome.

Small details, significant only as straws in the wind, were the facts that the street-lighting system in Rome and the practice of vaccination were abandoned by the new wholly clerical government as "revolutionary novelties," and that the Jews of Rome were again confined to the ghetto and three hundred of them were rounded up by the police every Sunday to hear a sermon. It is also a matter of more than a little importance that, while one early nineteenth century pope had a large family of illegitimate children, the church somewhat tardily discovered that its prestige might be improved by an improvement of papal morals, and subsequent popes have not been open to criticism on that score.

THE VATICAN COUNCIL

The year 1870 saw the two events which, more than any others in many centuries, determine the present status of the popes. On July 18, the Vatican Council voted, and Pius IX pronounced, the decree of the infallibility of the pope. Two months later, on September 20, the army of Victor Emmanuel marched through a breach in the walls of Rome and the thousand years of papal temporal sovereignty came to an end.

The Vatican Council was a most extraordinary and interesting assembly. If it was "unique in the number of bishops assembled," it was also unique in the exclusion of the laity. It was the first general council in which there was no lay representation. Eastern Orthodox and Protestants were invited, but it turned out that these invitations were meant to hold good only if they came acknowledging the authority of the Roman Catholic church and the supremacy of the pope—as it was known that they would not. The council was expected to produce a new counter-reformation, to defeat all heresies, perhaps even to heal all schisms. And above all it was intended to approve of a formal declaration of papal infallibility.

Some Catholic writers argue that the council was not specifically intended to take action on this point. (e. g., Rev. Richard Downey, in "The Papacy," Proceedings of the Cambridge Summer School of Catholic Studies.) It is true that when Pius IX in 1864 asked a group of cardinals for their opinion as to the wisdom of holding a council and the topics with which it should deal, only two of the twenty-one addressed made any mention of papal infallibility. But it is also true that he did not call the council until he had broached the subject of a proclamation of infallibility in an allocution to five hundred bishops assembled to celebrate the eighteenth centennial of the martyrdom of St.

Peter, June 26, 1867. When the bishops approved, the pope gave notice that he would call the council. He did so by the encyclical, *"Aeterni Patris Unigenitus Filius,"* on June 29, 1868. The flow of literature on the subject of papal infallibility began at once. Many learned ecclesiastics opposed the declaration, some on principle, others because they thought the proclamation of the dogma unwise and inopportune.

The council met Dec. 8, 1869, in the right transept of St. Peter's, which had been temporarily walled off for the purpose. A terrific storm made the bad acoustics worse.

The council was free from political influences, as earlier councils generally had not been, but it was subject to the control of the Vatican to an unparalleled degree. The pope selected the topics to be discussed, chose the committees to draw up the "schemata" in advance, appointed the chairmen of the four commissions into which the council was divided and the president of the *"congregationes generales,"* or committee of the whole, and handed out favors to those who favored infallibility and slights to those who did not. The opposing arguments could not be printed in Rome. Archbishop Kendrick of St. Louis, for example, had to send to Naples to have a pamphlet printed. The rules of procedure, dictated by the pope, required only a majority vote, not substantial unanimity as heretofore. The *"quod ab omnibus"* criterion seemed to be in abeyance for the moment. It was easier to decree a divine dogma in the Vatican Council than to nominate a candidate in a Democratic national convention. More than one hundred prelates signed a protest against this bare-majority rule, but protests were unavailing. All discussions were conducted in secret sessions, the stenographic reports of which are still locked up in the secret archives of the Vatican. There were copious leaks, however, even semi-official ones, so that the transactions are fairly well known.

That the matter was not rushed through is indicated by Downey: "For two months the constitution, *De Romani Pontificis Infallibili Magisterio,* treating of the primacy and infallibility of the pope, was discussed in all its bearings. The consideration of the fourth chapter, which treats explicitly of papal infallibility, occupied eleven sessions, during which fifty-seven speeches were delivered. The whole matter was threshed out with a thoroughness which has few parallels in the annals of debate." Later, in another connection, the same writer says: "One fact emerges clear—that the question as to whether the doctrine of papal infallibility be true or not was never discussed, was never even proposed for discussion. Within the council the whole question was as to the expediency and the terms of the definition."

It seems, then, that the council talked for two months about everything in connection with the new dogma except as to whether or not it was true. Why did they not discuss that? Two reasons are conceivable. Either they were all in agreement as to the truth of the dogma, or they were not allowed to discuss it. The evidence does not support the claim that they were all in agreement. And in connection with Downey's statement that the truth of the doctrine "was not even proposed for discussion," it is to be remembered that the pope himself decided what was to be discussed.

HOW INFALLIBILITY WAS VOTED

At the secret session on July 13, 1870, the matter was brought to a vote. With 601 present, 451 voted Yes; 88 voted No; 62 voted Yes with amendments (*placet juxta modum*). Something over 80 members of the council who were in or near Rome stayed away from the session to avoid voting. That evening the minority sent a deputation to the pope to beg him not to jeopardize the unity of the church by insisting upon being declared infallible. He did not yield.

On July 16 a phrase was added to make it clear that the infallibility of the pope did not depend upon or proceed from the consent of the church (*"non autem ex consensu ecclesiae"*). The minority was even more deeply distressed. Cardinal Rauscher urged the pope to consent to some softening of the doctrine. He replied, "It is too late."

The final vote in the public session was set for July 18. On the day before, 56 bishops sent to the pope a written protest, saying that they were unalterably opposed but would return to their dioceses to avoid public opposition. "Loyal piety and reverence do not permit us to vote No in your very face on a matter so intimately touching the person of your Holiness." That evening these 56 and 60 others left Rome. The following day the last formal session was held and the final vote was taken. There were 535 present. The vote stood 533 Yes, 2 No. Again, as at the opening session, there was a violent storm, and it grew so dark that the pope had to have a candle held at his shoulder to read out the decree of his own infallibility.

Commenting upon the beautiful consensus of opinion, the pope's official organ, *Civiltà Cattolica*, said: "What a wise direction of Providence! Only two Nays; therefore almost total unanimity. And yet, two Nays; therefore full liberty of the council. How vain are all attacks against the ecumenical character of this most beautiful of all councils!" The argument is all right if one can forget the one hundred and sixteen who left the night before to avoid voting.

The protesting bishops yielded to pressure one by one when the action had been irrevocably taken. Against such a dogma, once it had been made official, the only possible protest would have been secession from the church, and they were not prepared to secede. Why not? Because they did not dare, or because it would have meant too costly a sacrifice of the power, prestige and perquisites of ecclesiastical office? It is not necessary to make either assumption. Rather, because they believed in the Catholic theory of the church and so were accustomed to what an Italian writer of the period called the "sacrifice of the intellect"—meaning that the judgment of the individual must yield to the corporate judgment of the church.

And besides, we have the testimony of Lord Acton that the opposing bishops yielded "because they were persuaded that an irresistible reaction was at hand, and that the decrees of the Vatican Council would fade away and be dissolved by a power mightier than the episcopate and a process less perilous than schism. Their disbelief in the validity of their work was so profound that they were convinced that it would perish without violence and they resolved to spare the pope and themselves the indignity of a rupture." (Lord Acton: The History of Freedom and other Essays, p. 549.)

Even the two bishops who had dared to vote No yielded. They were Bishop Riccio of Cajazza, Sicily, and Bishop Fitzgerald of Little Rock, Arkansas.

Lord Acton, himself a Catholic and perhaps the most learned historian in Europe at the time, opposed the issuing of the decree of infallibility and the Constitution *Pastor Aeternus* put forth by the Vatican Council as a complete summary of Roman Catholic doctrine with reference to the pope. While the matter was still under discussion and the vote upon it was in imminent prospect, he wrote: "It makes civil legislation on all points of contract, marriage, education, clerical immunities, mortmain, even on many questions of taxation and common law, subject to the legislation of the church, which would be simply the arbitrary will of the pope. Most assuredly, no man accepting such a code could be a loyal subject or fit for the enjoyment of political privileges." (Correspondence, I, 103) But when the decree was issued, he made a formal submission to it.

The dogma was proclaimed by the pope on his own authority. It is not to be understood that the vote of the council either conferred infallibility upon the pope or definitely guaranteed that he already possessed it. A council may err. The councils of Pisa and Constance, for example, in the fifteenth century decreed that supreme authority is vested in a general council and that the decision of a pope is not final without its confirmation. So it would not do to rest the dogma of papal infallibility now upon the word of a council.

The full text of the decree is as follows:

Therefore, faithfully adhering to the tradition received from the beginning of the Christian faith, for the glory of God our Savior, the exaltation of the Catholic religion, and the salvation of Christian people, the Sacred Council approving, we teach and define that it is a dogma divinely revealed: that the Roman Pontiff, when he speaks ex cathedra—that is, when, in the discharge of the office of pastor and teacher of all Christians, by virtue of his supreme Apostolic authority, he defines a doctrine regarding faith or morals to be held by the Universal Church—is, by the divine assistance promised to him in Blessed Peter, possessed of that infallibility with which the Divine Redeemer willed that His Church should be endowed for defining doctrine regarding faith or morals; and that therefore such definitions of the Roman Pontiff are irreformable of themselves, and not from the consent of the Church.

DO AS I SAY, NOT AS I DO

It ought to be especially noted by Protestants that this is not equivalent to an assertion that the pope can do no wrong. His personal character is not involved. It is not sinlessness, but infallibility within certain limits, that is claimed. Many of the popes have been holy men and many others have been wild characters even according to the easy standards of their own times. Catholic scholars admit this, though they avoid the topic in books intended for popular consumption. But that matter is not directly at issue here. The point is that a pope, whatever may be his personal character, becomes by virtue of his office the repository of the teaching authority which was divinely given to the church and the object of a special providence which prevents him from wrongly defining any doctrine of faith or morals. A pope may get his office by bribery, as many of them have, or by political intrigue, as many have, or by the dominant influence of a secular power, as many have; no matter how he gets it or what sort of person he is, infallibility goes with the office.

The delinquencies of certain notorious popes are not referred to for the sake of casting obloquy upon them or discredit upon the office, but merely to emphasize the distinction between impeccability and infallibility. One who does not accept the Roman Catholic theory of the church, and especially one who believes that the genius of Christianity does not require in every generation a human voice uttering inerrant finalities about faith and morals, will doubtless be repelled by the apparent incongruity between wickedness and infallibility united in the same individual.

The inherent improbability of such an arrangement seems too great to be overcome by the evidence of a few texts of dubious interpretation, said texts being validated as the inerrant word of God only by that same church whose authority as the infallible teacher of truth rests in turn upon the texts which it validates. Nevertheless, whether one likes the combination or not, it is perfectly evident that, if the church is to have humanly embodied infallibility at all, it can have it upon no other terms. It accepts the terms and affirms that the infallibility of the pope is dependent solely upon his office and not at all upon his character.

Again, it is to be noted that the pope is not declared to be infallible at all times, under all circumstances and for all purposes. He is "not infallible as a man, or as a theologian, or as a priest, or as a bishop; or even as pope when he does not speak *ex cathedra*, or on a matter of faith or morals, or with the intention of binding the whole church." (Downey) The pope's opinion as to what tomorrow's weather will be is worth no more than the opinion of any one else. If, in reply to a private inquiry, he states that he is of the opinion that Christ's "descent into Hell" was an element of his humiliation, one may believe it or not. If, as Bishop of Rome, he issues an administrative order for his own diocese, there is no divine guarantee of its wisdom. As a temporal sovereign, when he was one, his acts and policies may have been better or worse than those of secular princes.

Infallibility is strictly limited to those cases in which the deliverance is *ex cathedra*, concerning faith or morals, and intended to be binding on the whole church.

This is perhaps not quite so clear as it seems to be. There has never been any official definition of "*ex cathedra*." Literally, "from the chair," of course, meaning doubtless the seat of Peter, "*Apostolica Sedis*," not a piece of furniture. The term was never used in a decree before the Vatican Council, and from that day to this the pope has never said, I am now speaking *ex cathedra*, or I am not now speaking *ex cathedra*. The faithful must then depend either upon their own fallible judgment, or upon the decision of some authority which is confessedly fallible, to determine whether this condition of infallibility is satisfied.

The limitation of infallibility to the fields of faith and morals is also important but ambiguous. There is a broad borderland of topics that lie between politics, for example, and morality; or perhaps one should say an area of double jurisdiction, where the teacher of morality and the maker of laws both properly claim a hearing. There is at least the possibility of embarrassment if one of the two claims to be infallible. On this point more will be said later in discussing church and state. But it must be noted even here that the assumption—which often rises into an assertion—that there is a clear and unmistakable line between matters of faith and morals and matters of secular and civic duty, is entirely groundless. For practical purposes, this limit upon papal infallibility means that the pope declares that he will not speak the word which must be received as infallible except upon questions which *he thinks* are related to faith and morals, and that if he thinks a given question belongs in that class the faithful must think so too; for it would be absurd to ascribe infallibility to an authority in a given field while doubting its competence to decide what questions lie in that field.

Catholics who, by way of proving their good citizenship, say that they would refuse to obey a command of the pope if it invaded the area which the state should control, are speaking very bravely but very carelessly.

As illustrations of this willingness of some Catholics to profess a degree of independence in judging whether an ecclesiastical pronouncement is properly in the field of the church's authority or invalid because outside of it, take the following oft quoted statement from an address delivered by Archbishop Ireland in Milwaukee, Aug. 11, 1913: "To priest, to bishop, or to pope, who—I am willing to consider the hypothesis—should attempt to rule in matters civil and political, to influence the citizen beyond the range of their own orbit of jurisdiction—that of the things of God, the answer is quickly made: 'Back to your own sphere of rights and duties—back to the things of God!'" Or, for a more recent instance, Father J. Elliott Ross, speaking in March, 1927, before a forum under the auspices of the Knights of Columbus in New York:

"The supreme law for Catholics is conscience, even over the orders of the pope. The pope's governing power is limited to religion, and there is conflict between church and state only upon the condition that one side invades the sphere of the other. If the state invades the principles of the church, Catholics are not bound to obey. If the pope should transgress the realm of pure politics, there too Catholics must not obey." And Father Ross himself says that the authority of the pope forms "the essential difference between Catholicity and all other forms of Christianity."

The resultant of all these statements, including the most liberal of them, seems to be that Catholics are not bound to obey the pope in *purely* political matters, but that they are bound to accept his decision as to whether any given question belongs to the realm of politics or of religion.

For a Catholic to take issue with the pope as to whether a decree of his was within his field of authority, would be an act of rebellion. There are many, doubtless, who would not shrink from it in an extreme case.

THE POPE WINS

There was much dissatisfaction within the church over the decree of infallibility, but it came to nothing. Döllinger, who had been for forty years a Catholic professor of theology at Munich, led the protest and was promptly excommunicated. His followers, who were most numerous in Germany, Austria and German

Switzerland, organized the Old Catholic church. But
the elements which were united in protest were divided
in their programs of action, and the movement soon
became merely a respectable small episcopal denomi-
nation of no epochal importance.

The two influences which, more than any others
(aside from straight ecclesiastical pressure), tended
to destroy the opposition were the war upon the Catholic church in Germany, and especially in Prussia,
known as the Kulturkampf, and the taking of Rome
by Victor Emmanuel. Bismarck's hostile measures
against the church, the Falk Laws of 1873, were so
unjust and the enforcement of them so drastic, that
Catholic sentiment was consolidated. The minds of
the discontented were taken off of any grievance they
may have had against the Vatican Council and Pius
IX, and they were given a new and more substantial
grievance against the government. Bismarck never
realized the gravity of the issues. He treated them
as a politician always treats other people's principles,
as going no deeper than his own policies of expediency.
He drove moderate Catholics to ultramontanism, gave
them martyrs and a cause to fight for, left them with
a well developed press (over one hundred Catholic
papers instead of three or four, within ten years),
made them the Center political party and the strongest element in German politics for the rest of the century. Nothing succeeds—for the persecuted—like
persecution, provided it stops short of complete an-
nihilation.

Apparent persecution does almost as well. Napoleon's strong-arm methods with Pius VII were considerably exaggerated in popular report, but fact and fiction together did much to win sympathy and support for the pope in that emergency. So when Pius IX lost his temporal sovereignty and became a "prisoner" in the Vatican within a few weeks after the declaration of his infallibility, sympathy played a part in winning acceptance for the dogma. Perhaps also it seemed safer to allow him absolute spiritual authority now that he was no longer an earthly ruler. It was, for example, obviously a gesture of compensation when the King of Italy, before he had gotten the carpets down in the palace which he had taken from the pope, suppressed the "Appeal to the Catholic Bishops," in which Döllinger spoke of "the overthrow of two despotisms, the empire of the Napoleons and the temporal power of the papacy," and appealed to the bishops to repudiate the dogma which established a new spiritual despotism.

ITALY ANNEXES ROME

The popes had been the sovereigns of Rome and a territory of varying size adjacent to it for more than a thousand years. The "donation" of Constantine is fiction; Lorenzo Valla proved that as early as 1450, and the only reply that has ever been made to his argument is the charge (a true one) that Lorenzo was an immoral person. But at least from the time of Gregory the Great, about the year 600, the bishops of

Rome had great landed estates, as many other bishops had, and from the time of Pippin and Charlemagne the popes ruled over a territory to which they had as good a title as any prince had to his dominion.

The revolutionary movements which broke out all over Europe early in the nineteenth century affected the various states in Italy no less than other countries, and the States of the Church no less than the other Italian states and for the same reason—namely, that the government was antiquated, autocratic and tyrannical. Since the hand of Austria lay heavy upon Italy and since the papal state was probably the worst governed part of the country, the new patriotism which, from the time of Mazzini, began to demand a free and united Italy, found its favorite objects of attack in Austrian interference and papal sovereignty. Within two years after his accession, Pius had to flee from Rome in disguise, a constituent assembly voted that he had forfeited his sovereignty, and a short-lived Roman republic was set up in 1848. Venice and Tuscany also became republics, after expelling the Austrians. But Austria soon came back, the two northern republics fell, and a French army captured Rome and set up a government in the name of the pope, who did not consider it safe to return until the following year.

Victor Emmanuel, King of Piedmont and Sardinia, the protagonist of Italian liberty and unity, clung to three ideas: to free Italy from the domination of Austria; to unite it under the leadership of Piedmont;

and to make his own government worthy of that position of leadership by making it a model constitutional
monarchy. With Piedmont as a nucleus, the new
Kingdom of Italy gradually came to justify that name
by the successive additions of Tuscany, Parma, Mo-
dena, Romagna, Naples, Umbria, and finally, in 1866,
Venice. These were not conquests but unions supported by popular votes. The capital was moved from
Turin to Florence. Nothing remained for the comple-
tion of the task of uniting Italy except the addition
of Rome, the inevitable capital; and nothing prevented
the annexation of Rome except the protection of the
papal regime by a French army.

The very days of the votes and protests in the
Vatican Council regarding papal infallibility (July
13-18) were the days of mobilization for the war of
1870 between France and Prussia. The German mobilization orders were given on the night of July 15.
With the outbreak of this war, the French troops were
necessarily withdrawn from Rome, and the days of
papal sovereignty were numbered.

The war was short and decisive. Ten days after
the battle of Sedan, the army of Victor Emmanuel
entered the Papal State. Honorable terms were offered
to the pope—independence, income, palaces, dignity,
ambassadorial privileges—but he replied *"non possu-
mus."* He would not capitulate until an actual breach
was made in the walls of Rome. So a breach was
made, as gently as possible to avoid doing any damage
or hurting anybody, at a spot now marked by three

memorial tablets and a column of victory near the
Porta Pia, and the white flag was run up, Sept. 20,
1870.

The Law of Guarantees, dated May 13, 1871, declared papal sovereignty over the States of the Church
at an end and substituted therefor certain privileges
and assurances: the use and occupancy of the palace
and grounds of the Vatican, St. John Lateran, Castel
Gondolfo, an income of 3,225,000 lire (about $600,-
000), the right of maintaining a private guard and of
sending and receiving ambassadors, and certain personal immunities. Two days later Pius IX denounced
and rejected this law, refused to accept the stipend,
and declared himself a prisoner in the Vatican. He
"condemned, rescinded, annulled, and abrogated" all
acts of the government connected with this "sacrilege
and spoliation," and said: "We declare and protest before God and the whole Catholic world that we are
thrown into such captivity that we cannot freely and
completely exercise our supreme pastoral authority."
As this was only three months after the declaration
of infallibility, it may be presumed that such a solemn
statement would not have been made—whether *"ex
cathedra"* or not—except with the intention of establishing a fixed policy of the church.

THE POPES PROTEST

All the popes from then until now have reaffirmed
their demand for the status of independent sovereignty.
Leo XIII denounced the Law of Guarantees and ex-

communicated the King of Italy as a usurper. Pius X, on Dec. 18, 1903, wrote: "It is the duty of Catholic journalists to keep alive in the minds of the people the conviction that the Holy See finds itself in an intolerable position since the invasion of its civil principality." Benedict XV, in the encyclical *"Pacem,"* May 23, 1920, permitting Catholic sovereigns to visit Rome and have friendly relations with the King of Italy, re-asserted his claim to sovereignty. On Sept. 2, 1921, *L'Osservatore Romano,* the official Vatican organ, said: "The legitimacy of the papal possession is incontestable. It was suppressed only on the theory that might makes right. The Holy See has always protested against the spoliation, nor can it renounce any part of that territory which under the present circumstances remains necessary as a guarantee of the liberty and independence of its ministry." Last of all, the present pope, Pius XI, reaffirmed the demand for sovereignty in the encyclical *"Ubi Arcano,"* Dec. 23, 1922, and in a brief issued in February, 1926.

Why are the popes so insistent upon the prerogative of temporal power? Solely that they may have absolute freedom for the exercise of their spiritual functions, they say. To quote the Archbishop of Udine, speaking for Pius X at a clerical assembly at Milan, Dec. 1, 1913: "The liberty of the pope must be full and complete with respect to all the acts pertaining to his spiritual and universal ministry. It is not enough to secure the inviolability of the pope's person and those of his ministry, or extraterritoriality, or a postal frank. Full liberty means that all must have access to the pope at all times without hindrance and must be able to communicate with him at any time and under any circumstances, in peace and in war. Moreover, the liberty of the pope must not be precarious, but must be stable and unalterable. It must be such that no power can violate it with impunity *or even be a judge of the measure of that independence*. This independence therefore ought to be supported by an international guarantee."

All of which means not only that spiritual ministries ought to be free from the interference of the civil state—which is a good principle that no Protestant nowadays will deny—but also that when differences of opinion arise, as they easily may, as to whether a given action constitutes a spiritual ministry, or is essential to it, the church should be the one to decide. No secular power must "even be a judge of the measure of that independence." The natural and logical corollary of such papal independence from any state control is the independence of all his agents and all the clergy—who are likewise engaged in a spiritual ministry—from civil laws and civil courts. Time was when priests and monks could be tried only in courts maintained by the church, and Pius IX, in his Syllabus of Errors in 1864, was still inveighing against the abolition of this "privilege of clergy" as an error. We hear of no present campaign for the restoration of these ecclesiastical courts, but it would be strictly consistent with the demand for temporal sovereignty as a necessary condition of papal liberty.

A more substantial advantage from the regaining of sovereignty would be the enhanced prestige of the Catholic church, and its increased facilities for diplomatic access to civil governments. Already nearly all the important countries exchange ambassadors with the Vatican. Italy and the United States are the most significant exceptions. At most of the capitals, the papal representative is *ex officio* dean of the diplomatic corps and enjoys precedence. With the Papal State reconstituted and admitted to the League of Nations, it requires little imagination to picture the pope being put forward as the permanent president of the Council. McClorey concludes his recent book with a glowing picture of the pope as the peacemaker of the nations and the arbiter of the quarrels of the world. (McClorey: "The Church and the Republic," 1928.)

CAN PAPAL SOVEREIGNTY COME BACK?

What chance is there—if any—that the pope will get back the status of a civil ruler? Perhaps more than most people in America imagine. It is a live question, and it has taken on new urgency within the past few years. The Kingdom of Italy absolutely must have Rome as its capital. No one can well deny that, if there is to be a Kingdom of Italy at all. Suggestions involving the transfer of the seat of the papacy to some other place are absurd. Corfu, Avignon, Sicily and Corsica have been suggested. Some enthusiastic Americans even proposed to erect a papal state on a large tract in Louisiana, though how they expected to get sovereign possession of it was not divulged. But the papacy cannot be transplanted. By its own definition, the Catholic church is "Catholic, Apostolic and *Roman.*" The solution of the Roman question, if there is to be one, must be found at Rome.

The approach to it was opened up when, in 1916, when the war was going rather well for Germany, and Italy was on the other side, the Jesuit Franz Ehrle, who was later made a cardinal by Pius XI, published a monograph in the German Catholic review, *Stimmen der Zeit,* proposing the creation of a *small* papal state. About the same time, the German Imperial Chancellor made official announcement before the Bavarian parliament that Germany and her allies had negotiations on foot for the creation of a pontifical state. A Catholic member of the German cabinet, Erzberger, in his "Memoirs," states the terms which were agreed upon. The gist of them was that Italy was to be compelled to cede to the pope a small territory on the north bank of the Tiber, whose independence and neutrality should be guaranteed by all the contracting powers, and to pay to the Holy See an indemnity of five hundred million lire. But the outcome of the war put an end to that scheme.

In 1921, a new attitude began to be manifest in the secular Italian press. The leading nationalistic paper of Rome, *"Il Messagero,"* asserted that Italy "had emerged from the war strong enough now to be able to face the problem" of a satisfactory settlement with the pope. Several other papers followed with editorials pitched in the same key, and the minister of foreign affairs took cognizance of the change of sentiment to the extent of publishing in a pamphlet selections from these editorials together with three speeches delivered in the chamber of deputies, one of them by Mussolini, then a member of the chamber. It was shortly after this, on Sept. 2, 1921, that *"L'Osservatore Romano"* printed its editorial, already quoted, hinting that the Holy See might be willing to accept some modification of its former territorial claims. The "small state" idea was brought forward again.

On June 2, 1922, the Roman newspaper, *"Il Tempo,"* urged the necessity of giving the pope absolute sovereignty over some territory, however slight— "even a single square centimeter." Three days later *"Il Messagero"* asserted that the question had gotten off of the dead center upon which it had been stalled for half a century, and proposed the revision of the Law of Guarantees, the substitution of a bi-lateral contract for a uni-lateral law, and the giving of absolute sovereignty to the pope over the Vatican and its grounds. A small principality, to be sure, but considerably larger than the "single square centimeter" suggested three days before.

Jean Carrère, Rome correspondent of the Paris *"Le Temps,"* published in 1924 a book entitled "The Pope," in which he argued strongly for the historic

right and present necessity of "the sovereign possession of a territorial domain by which the pope is completely removed from the jurisdiction and surveillance
of any human power whatsoever." He makes his contribution to the "small state" plan: "The new principality might be extended northeast as far as the Villa
Pamphili, which it might absorb, and southwest as
far as that melancholy *Pineta Sacchetti* which may be
seen from the top of the Janiculum, as one looks beyond St. Peter's to a hill of considerable height where,
like a natural colonnade, a harmonious forest of pines
rises against the sky . . . Others dream of a rather
wider kingdom, reaching to the sea by a strip of land,
at the extremity of which a new port might be constructed. That would permit the Holy See to have its
window freely open to the whole world. Finally others
—but let us stop."

Yes, perhaps it is best to stop there. The directions seem somewhat mixed, but so far as I can make
out, the "melancholy pineta sacchetti" marks the sum-
mit of Monte Mario, the site lately purchased by the
Methodists and now occupied by their Collegio Inter-
nazionale.

THE FASCISTI AND THE CHURCH

The prospect of some sort of settlement of the
"Roman question" rests chiefly upon the increased
friendliness of the government to the church under the
Fascisti regime, and that in turn rests upon the reali-
zation of the value of religion—that is, Catholicism—

as a bond of national unity. Every important movement in Italy for a thousand years has been colored
and emotionalized by a sense of the heritage of the
ancient Roman glories. Part of that historic heritage,
and the most conspicuously visible part, is the Roman
Catholic church. Fascismo undertook to use the
church as a means of building morale and exalting
national pride. Like the church, it is a movement in
reaction against democracy and modern tendencies. It
is, says Curzio Suchert, "the reaction of the Latin
mind and of Catholicism against the aberrations and
degeneracies of the modern spirit. The ascendency of
modern thought, born with the Protestant Reformation
and developed through the French Revolution, is now
at an end."

Yet even the "small state" movement seems to be
checked for the moment. An interchange of opinions
between *"L'Osservatore Romano"* and the official Fas-
cist publication in October, 1927, left it clear that,
while the church was still insisting upon the right of
the pope to a temporal domain, it would consider a
very small territory sufficient for its purposes, but the
government asserted without qualification that it could
not consider the alienation of even "a single square
centimeter."

The negotiations have been continued, however,
informally but seriously, with the Jesuit Tacchi-
Venturi as go-between. Press reports in February,
1928—as to the accuracy of which I know no more
than any other newspaper reader—assert that a

virtual agreement has been reached upon three points: the ceding to the pope of a considerable tract of land, including the magnificent Villa Doria-Pamphili with its extensive grounds, without sovereignty but with the same rights of extraterritoriality which are now attached to the property occupied by the pope; the paying of a very large "indemnity" by the government to the pope, estimated at about $400,000,-000; and the making of a new concordat between church and state, regulating their future relations, and notifying the world through diplomatic channels that such agreements have been concluded and that the pope's freedom of action under all conceivable circumstances has been guaranteed by the government.

This approach to a settlement of the Roman question also appears to be blocked, temporarily at least, by the conflict between the Vatican and the Fascisti government on the subject of education and Catholic youth organizations (April, 1928).

The proposed indemnity is the feature of this suggested settlement which will doubtless be the first to elicit comment, especially in a country which has recently granted Italy an extraordinary reduction of her war debts on account of her supposed inability to pay. The amount of the proposed indemnity is probably arrived at by calculating what the allowance of 3,225,-000 lire a year, granted in 1871 but never accepted, would amount to by this time with accumulated interest. As the principal comes to only about $34,000,000, it is obvious that the interest must have been reckoned at a very much higher rate than the one and a fraction percent that Italy is now paying on her debt to the United States.

The presupposition upon which this indemnity is based is that the States of the Church constituted not merely a territory ruled by the church—that is to say, by the pope—but a piece of property belonging to him. One shudders to think what would happen to the treasuries of the various European governments if they undertook to pay similar indemnities to every dynasty that has been dispossessed in the last hundred years. The loss of Rome by the popes was not wholly, if at all, an act of spoliation committed by an outside power. Perhaps the results of the plebiscite taken in Rome after its occupation by the army of united Italy —40,788 for the king and 40 for the pope—are not to be taken too seriously, for the pope ordered his adherents not to vote. But it is a well established fact that the kind of government which the popes had conducted in their domain during the preceding half century—to go back no farther—had no chance to survive against the growing demand for freedom and representation. The popes lost Rome partly because Italy wanted it for its capital, and partly because they had given it an outrageously tyrannical and autocratic government. If they get any such tremendous "indemnity" now, they will be luckier than the heirs-at-law of any of the other monarchs whose despotisms were submerged in the rising tide of democracy.

IV

TRANSPLANTED TO AMERICA

American Catholicism is not some new and liberal development from the old stock. It is the old stock itself. This statement refers, of course, to the system—its principles, its organization, its hierarchy, its centralized and wholly clerical control—and not to the cultural and political characteristics of its laity. Some new policies have been adopted to meet the new conditions, for never before did Catholicism exist in a state which gave it equal rights and full liberty but no favors. Repudiating the status of a sect among sects, it has nevertheless had to live as though it were just that. From the headquarters in Rome have come frequent reassertions of its uniqueness and of its right to preferential treatment by the government, yet it has had to make the best of a situation in which legal equality was the best it could hope for. This has produced some embarrassments but, on the whole, it has worked well for the church.

The Roman Catholicism which was transplanted from Europe to the new soil of America was a Catholicism which had reached and passed the zenith of its visible power. It had felt the convulsion of the Protestant insurrection, and had begun to brace itself for a struggle by a series of internal adjustments, reaffirmations of doctrine and a few reforms. This reaction against the first surge of Protestantism, which at first seemed likely to capture all Europe, is known as the Counter-reformation. We cannot, in this treatise, spend much time on the events of long ago, but we must take one sweeping glance at the situation as it was before the map of the world was unrolled to disclose a new continent.

The latter part of the Middle Ages had brought Roman Catholicism to the pinnacle of its power and the finest flower of its intellectual life. Innocent III had carried the prestige and supremacy of the papacy to a point beyond which nothing more was possible. Thomas Aquinas had given the system of Catholic theology a philosophical setting and support so satisfactory to the ruling powers of the church that his work remains to this day the standard of correctness and the bulwark of Catholic doctrine against "modernism." The Gothic cathedral builders had provided a worthy architectural embodiment of Catholic devotion and aspiration. Dante had put it into unsurpassed poetry. The new religious orders, founded by St. Francis and St. Dominic, had added moral power and supplied an army of eager propagandists. There were rumblings of discontent, but the claims and the glories of Catholicism were never so great.

All these things happened in the thirteenth and fourteenth centuries. America was discovered in the fifteenth. It was therefore a completely Catholic Europe which caught the first glimpse of the new world. But before the first impulse to explore and exploit had passed over into an impulse to colonize, before it had occurred to anyone that the new lands were places where people might live as well as an obstacle on the searoad to the Indies and a place where gold could be gathered to fill the depleted treasuries of Europe, the incipient revolt had become actual and the Protestant reformation had begun.

THE POPE MAKES A GIFT HE CANNOT DELIVER

Of the five great maritime nations, two remained safely Catholic—Spain and Portugal; two became definitely Protestant—England and the Netherlands; France, seriously divided, was at war with itself but predominantly and officially Catholic. When Pope Alexander VI, himself a Spaniard, generously divided the new world between the two Catholic powers by what was perhaps the most flamboyant gesture of universal sovereignty that even a pope ever ventured, he drew the line of demarcation so far east that Portugal got only the great knee which South America thrusts out toward Africa. Spain got all the rest. Even Catholic France did not feel bound by that decree, and still less did the Protestant English and Dutch. All five of the great powers planted their flags where they could and colonized according to their needs and abilities.

While the main streams of influence and immigration which flowed into the territory destined to become the United States were Protestant, the Catholic elements were far from negligible. Of the first four permanent settlements north of the Rio Grande, three were Catholic: the Spanish at St. Augustine in 1565 and at Santa Fe in 1605 or 1606, the English at Jamestown in 1607, and the French at Quebec in 1608. Later Catholic enterprises which contributed permanent values in the colonial period were the French explorations and settlements in the Mississippi Valley, with a focal point at New Orleans, the Spanish conquest of California, and the English Catholic colony in Maryland.

There were fine, heroic elements in all of these movements, and the part which the Catholic clergy played in them supplies some of the brightest pages in American history. The part which the Catholic laity played supplies some of the darkest and bloodiest. The work of the French Jesuits, chiefly in Canada but crossing by way of the Great Lakes into the Mississippi Valley, merits the high praise that all historians have given it. History records few nobler illustrations of intrepid exploration, self-sacrificing devotion and peaceful penetration into a hostile country in the interest of religion than those embodied in the many-volumed "Jesuit Relations." The Spanish priests in New Mexico in the seventeenth century furnished their quota to the roll of martyrs. The Franciscans in California in the eighteenth century, led by Junipero Serra, were true fathers to their people, keeping them perhaps unduly ignorant and dependent according to our standards but from motives whose purity can be questioned only by the most captious critics.

MISSIONARIES AND MARAUDERS

The best of these priests were sincere lovers of the souls of men. The two objectives, of saving souls and advancing the glory of the church, presented no alternative to their minds. Souls were to be saved only by imposing the authority of the church, and the glory of the church was to be enhanced by extending its dominion and saving souls. Why should a Protestant seek to discredit them by saying that they cared only to magnify the church and exalt its power, when the two motives were indistinguishably mingled in their thought?

By all these agencies and others a large factor of Catholic thought and practice was planted in the regions where presently a different set of religious ideas and loyalties were to be introduced. And while priests were living and, in some cases, dying for their faith, other men, also Catholics, were seeking plunder and conquest at whatever cost to the aborigines. There was the same contrast here that there was in the regions occupied by the Protestants, and that there always is between the attitudes of those who go among weaker peoples to do them good and those who go to exploit them. Catholic writers attempt to make a case for the church by contrasting the careers of Jesuits like Marquette with those of "Protestant" Indian-fighters. There is nothing in it. One may as well reverse the picture by comparing John Eliot, the Protestant apostle to the Indians, with the perfidious and bloody Pizarro.

THE ECONOMIC INFLUENCE

How about these charges of "Spanish Catholic cruelty" on the one hand and "Anglo-Saxon Protestant ruthlessness" on the other in the treatment of the aborigines in the early days? There is too much truth in the charges on both sides to give either much advantage in a comparison.

The Spanish in Peru and Mexico wanted gold; the French in Canada wanted furs; the English in what became the United States wanted land.

Getting gold meant stealing it from those who had it, with concomitant slaughter of the owners, or slave labor in the mines. Hence cruelty. Getting furs required sufficiently friendly relations with the Indians so that they would bring in furs to the trading posts. Cruelty would have sent them back into the wilderness to stay and would have defeated the purpose of the enterprise. Hence kindness, copiously mixed with cheating—if you can call it cheating to give a savage a worthless thing that he wants in exchange for a valuable thing that he doesn't want. Getting land required either purchase, as in the rare case of Penn, or diplomacy backed by fire-arms, as in New England, or simply driving the Indians from their hunting grounds, as was the general practice.

The Anglo-Saxons encountered Indians who lived

by hunting. A hunting party looks, and often acts, like a war party. Besides, hunters must have a monopoly of their area. Try to establish squatter sovereignty and put in a crop on the grounds of a duck-club or within the limits of a private game preserve, and see how welcome you will be. Hence mutual suspicion and conflict of interests.

Here, if ever, the economic factor was the determining one. It was not primarily a question of either the race or the religion of the invaders, except perhaps in the case of the Quakers.

Neither Catholicism nor Protestantism, per se, fostered cruelty to the aborigines. Unfortunately also, neither of them fostered kindness, except in the case of a few really religious souls.

An illustration of the amenities of colonization where rival religions as well as rival nations were involved, is afforded by the massacre of the French Protestant colony in Florida by the Spanish. Four years before the founding of St. Augustine, an expedition was sent out by the Huguenot prime minister of France, Admiral Coligny, a settlement was made first in Port Royal Sound and later on St. John's River, and the flag of France was raised on land claimed by Spain under the bull of Alexander VI. This event precipitated the expedition of Menendez, for "not only France but Protestantism was in the very heart of the territory claimed by Spain. It behooved Spain to make a supreme effort, or see her supremacy in the New World threatened by a political and religious foe."

(O'Gorman: "History of the Roman Catholic Church in the United States.") Ten days after the planting of the Spanish flag at St. Augustine, the Spanish fleet made a hostile demonstration against the French colony, which was answered by a similar naval parade by the French before St. Augustine, without an actual attack in either case. While the French fleet was still scattered by a storm, Menendez made a swift dash to the defenseless colony, "found it unsentineled, and put to the sword 141 inmates—men, women and children. Father Mendoza, the parish priest of the new city, came forth in surplice, crucifix in hand, to meet the hero of the massacre. He, kneeling with his men, kissed the cross; then, arising, they entered the town amid the chant of the Te Deum." (O'Gorman) The survivors of the wrecked French fleet drifted ashore and unconditionally surrendered, after which "they were put to the sword, none being spared but a few Catholics among them."

All of which proves nothing in particular about the inhumanity of Catholics as Catholics, though the priestly blessing upon the massacre singularly parallels the pope's Te Deum after the massacre of St. Bartholomew's day. But it does take the edge off of what Shuster (in "The Catholic Spirit in America") says of "the callous advance of the Anglo-Saxon"—which was callous enough, no doubt, but scarcely rose to those heights of savagery which were attained by the Spanish in their treatment of both natives and Protestant colonists.

The relation of religion to buccaneering in the sixteenth and seventeenth centuries reveals equally little difference between the two confessions.

EVEN THE PIRATES WERE PIOUS

Drake, a gentle but very efficient robber who boasted that he never killed a man in his life but who plundered the Spanish when the two countries were at peace, was a very pious Protestant, read prayers regularly to his crew and sometimes preached.

De Lussan, a Catholic, "would not permit his murderous buccaneers to start looting until he had led them all to church and there heard mass said—after which ceremony the robbery and rapine would begin." (Wycherley: "Buccaneers of the Pacific." New York, 1927.)

William Patterson, Scotch and Protestant, came to the West Indies as a missionary, but decided that he could please God best by robbing and killing Catholic Spaniards.

Montbars, a fanatical French Catholic, read Las Casas, and became so furious at Spanish cruelty to the Indians that he devoted himself to the humanitarian enterprise of exterminating as many Spaniards as he could encounter, in spite of their common religion.

Jacques de Sores, French Huguenot, looted the Spanish Main without losing his faith.

Pizarro and Cortez were models of Catholic piety,

whose religion imposed no restraint upon their cruelty, lust and treachery.

A statistical balance would probably show that Catholics killed a good many more Indians than Protestants did, but it was chiefly because they were where the temptations and the opportunities were greater.

The history of Spain disproves such explanations as that of Father Knox ("The Belief of Catholics," p. 241) that the Catholic Church would never practice coercion except where "the non-Catholic minority are innovators, newly in revolt against the Catholic system, with no ancestral traditions, no vested interests to be respected." From the eighth to the fifteenth century, Spain was not a completely Catholic country. The Moors and Jews were there for hundreds of years, they were not newly in revolt, they had the strongest kind of ancestral traditions, and they had acquired all sorts of vested interests. There was general toleration and good will among Jews, Moors and Christians. No Spaniards went on the crusades to the Holy Land—or at least no great number—but the movement against the Moors by Ferdinand and Isabella was a belated parallel. The inquisition against heretics, started in 1480, was extended in 1492 to take in the Jews. They were given the choice of conversion or exile. After that, those who remained were presumed to have been converted and were treated as heretics if they failed to show the proper reactions. In Castile and Leon there were 50,000 forced conversions,

15,000 driven into exile, and 20,000 killed. The survivors, if any, were treated as heretics. This system was extended in 1500 to include the Moors who had lingered after the conquest.

A bishop of the 16th century—quoted in La Fuente's *Historia de España*—said that it was right to kill heretics, even one's own parents or children. That, of course, was only an extreme statement of an old doctrine. The interesting feature of the total episode is that a policy of coercion was adopted toward those who had a non-Catholic tradition of long standing.

IN COLONIAL DAYS

In the planting and development of the English colonies along the Atlantic seaboard, Catholics played a comparatively inconspicuous part. The only colony in which they were an important factor was Maryland, and even there they were in the minority. After a brief period of toleration—the credit for which will be discussed in a later chapter—the intolerance which was imported along with the religious prejudices and political fears of the old world settled down upon Maryland also. If Protestants could barely tolerate each other in that illiberal age, much less could they tolerate Catholics, who had always been intolerant of them. Religious liberty was a plant of slow growth. In general, Catholics labored under serious civil disabilities throughout the colonial period. Laymen were not often molested on account of their faith, but public Catholic worship was prohibited by law in several colonies though in most of them the law was not strictly enforced. Catholic priests were forbidden even to live in New York in the period immediately before the Revolution.

The most numerous and energetic group of priests in the English colonies, as well as in the French territory in the Mississippi valley which became British in 1763, were Jesuits. There were enough of these when the society was suppressed by papal bull in 1773 so that an arrangement was made by which "the suppressed Jesuits in Maryland and Pennsylvania were to form a body corporate which was to hold, until the restoration of the Society of Jesus, the property formerly held by the individuals of that society in those two colonies." (O'Gorman: "History of the Catholic Church in the United States," p. 265.) An interesting testimony to two facts: that Jesuits held property as individuals although they were forbidden by the rules of the order to do so; and that they did not loyally and submissively accept the bull of dissolution, which the pope declared to be irrevocable.

In view of the fewness of their numbers—estimated at 30,000 in all the colonies out of a total population of 3,000,000 at the time of the Revolution—and the restrictive laws to which they were subjected, it is not to be held against the Catholics as a group that they were but a small factor in the political and cultural life of the thirteen colonies in pre-revolutionary days. But the fact is that they did have a relatively unimportant place both before and in the Revolution.

The Catholic stars in the struggle for independence were Charles Carroll of Carrollton, one of the signers of the Declaration of Independence, and his brother, the priest, John Carroll, who became in 1787 the first American bishop. Both of these were sent, with Benjamin Franklin and Samuel Chase, on a mission to Canada in 1776 to attempt to secure the adherence of Canada to the American cause. Their failure was at least partly due to Catholic Canada's unfavorable impression of the hostility of the American colonies to Catholicism. The suspicions of disloyalty which attached to Catholics during the Revolution on account of their connection with their co-religionists in Canada, appear to have been without foundation.

Exaggerated claims are sometimes made as to the services rendered by Catholics in laying the foundations of the republic. The conclusions which seem to the present writer to be supported by the known facts are: *first,* that Catholics played a minor part but one fairly proportional to their numbers; *second,* that it was on the whole an honorable part; *third,* that their contribution was not dependent upon the distinctive features of the Catholic system of either faith or government. Catholics, numbering about one percent of the population, probably bore one percent of the responsibility and the burden of winning freedom from England. Catholicism contributed nothing to that cause.

Until 1784 the administration of the affairs of the church in the American colonies was under the vicar apostolic of London. An effort to have it transferred to French hands was successfully opposed, and in that year John Carroll was appointed prefect apostolic, under the Congregation of the Propaganda. Five years later he became Bishop of Baltimore, the first American bishop. He had been a Jesuit until the suppression of the order in 1773. For nearly twenty years he was the only American bishop—using the term "American" in the narrower sense—and had jurisdiction over the church throughout the territory of the United States. Complicated machinations of church politicians, strongly opposed by Bishop Carroll, attempted to fasten French and Irish control upon the American church. "It looked in the first quarter of the century as if home rule were to be taken from the church in the United States through foreign interference," says O'Gorman. To what extent this effort succeeded, opinions will differ. It has always seemed to Protestants that the element of foreign control was considerable, but it is significant that the first bishop was of American birth and undoubted patriotism, in spite of the fact that he left America at the age of twelve and did not return until he was forty.

THE CHURCH AND THE IMMIGRANTS

The acquisition of the eastern half of the Mississippi Valley, under the treaty which ended the Revolutionary War, gave the new nation a great inland territory which had lately belonged to France and in which the foundations, such as they were, had been laid by Catholics. The Louisiana purchase added more French Catholic settlements, notably St. Louis and New Orleans. In 1793 the diocese of New Orleans was established and in 1808 the sees of New York, Philadelphia, Boston and Bardstown, Ky. Since then the organization has increased in proportion to the enlargement of the territory and the increase in population. In 1928 there are 99 Catholic bishops and 17 archbishops in the United States, administering 104 dioceses and archdioceses, and controlling 24,990 clergy.

The great growth of the Catholic church in America has been by immigration. The earliest large stream came from Ireland, increasing notably after 1820 and still more after the potato famine of 1845. The Irish became then, and have remained, the largest single factor in American Catholicism. German emigration was stimulated by the unsuccessful revolutionary movements of 1830 and 1848, but the Irish remained dominant. To a critic who pointed out that a disproportionate number of Catholics became public charges in poorhouses and hospitals, a Catholic writer replied, in 1856, that this was because "the exposed situations in labor are always filled by foreigners, principally Irish," and that these are mainly Catholic.

Anti-Catholic movements have, for the most part, been based upon the charge that the church is essentially foreign in its spirit, allegiance, and membership, and that it aims at political control through the domination of its masses of un-Americanized immigrants. The Federal party, it will be remembered, was suspicious of aliens. During John Adams' administration the president was empowered to expel suspected aliens and the period of residence required for naturalization was extended to fourteen years. Foreign-born Catholics in New York were required to take a special oath before exercising the rights of citizenship. Other states also retained some remnants of the discriminatory legislation of colonial days.

ANTI-CATHOLIC MOVEMENTS

Not long after the beginning of the first considerable stream of Irish immigration, about 1820, the rural Protestant Anglo-Saxons who made up the bulk of the population, and who naturally considered themselves the norm of Americanism, began to witness a new and alarming phenomenon—the massing together in the cities of thousands of new citizens with social and religious traditions radically different from their own. These new citizens entered into politics with the fervor characteristic of their race. It was suspected that they were subject to the orders of their priests—most of whom, like themselves, were of recent foreign origin—because it was known that their religious system gave the priesthood great power. Whether from the natural cohesion of racial solidarity or from priestly control, the "Catholic vote" seemed to form a bloc. In the cities, the competition of foreign labor was already being felt; all the more because there were as yet no effective labor unions.

A political party was organized in New York in 1834 with the two objects of requiring 21 years of residence before naturalization and "abridging the rapidly increasing political influence of the papal power in the United States." I do not know that any evidence was presented that political power was being exercised directly by the pope. "Papal power" probably meant the power of Catholics, which undoubtedly was increasing because they were becoming more numerous. There were a third of a million of them in 1830, and nearly a million in 1840, almost all in the cities; and since the total percentage of urban population was small, the increase of the Catholic vote in the cities was conspicuous. It was alleged that many immigrants—that is, Catholics—soon became dependents—"indigent and diseased"—"conveyed from the wharf on which they landed direct to the almshouse"— and that "crime of every degree increased five-fold and the prisons were peopled with exotic felons." Strong-arm methods were used in politics. There was disorder and intimidation at the polls, the Irish— Catholics, of course—playing a prominent and turbulent part. Especially was there fear of "foreign control" of New York City—meaning control from abroad, though the actual evidence pertained only to control by recent arrivals from abroad. The two ideas were easily confused in panicky minds, especially since most of these foreign-born new citizens owed spiritual allegiance, and nobody knew how much besides, to a foreign spiritual autocrat.

So a political party was organized in New York City to combat these dangers, and Samuel F. B. Morse, as its candidate for mayor, received about half enough votes to have elected him. After this defeat, the party collapsed. It was the first manifestation of hundred-percentism, combining race prejudice with religious antagonism and labor unrest.

During the decade from 1835 to 1845 immigration, still largely Irish, continued to increase with accelerated velocity. The Catholic population practically doubled every ten years from 1790 to 1860, and by far the greater part of the increase came by immigration. Inevitably the increase of the priesthood came by immigration in about the same proportion. With increasing skill as well as added numbers, the political power of the Irish, especially in the eastern cities, became more impressive. It was the time of the great public school fight. The system of state elementary schools was in process of being established, and the Catholic church opposed the secularization of state-supported education in the hope of retaining or regaining state support for the parochial schools. It was a period of aggressive political action by the hierarchy in the United States in regard to these matters of disputed jurisdiction, though the assertions that its desire was to capture the government and direct it from Rome is backed by no convincing evidence.

It must be remembered, too, that at this period the papacy was in its most reactionary mood. Leo XII's encyclical of 1824 condemning religious toleration and liberty of conscience and anathematizing the Bible societies, and the 1826 "Letter to the clergy of Poitiers" declaring that "everyone who separates himself from the Roman Catholic church—God's wrath hangs over him," were recent enough to be well remembered. The papacy and Austria were allied enemies of the liberal and patriotic movement in Italy, and it was not difficult—although the Syllabus of Errors had not yet been issued—to find and quote utterances of highly placed Catholics which indicated an unfriendly attitude toward democracy in America.

Very likely these statements did not mean exactly what they were taken to mean. But, taking them all together, it is not surprising that many found cause for alarm in the tidal wave of immigrants of a faith professing these principles.

THE RISE AND FALL OF THE "KNOW-NOTHINGS"

The American Republican party came into existence in 1843, pledging itself to support for office no person "directly or indirectly subjected to or influenced by the laws or powers, temporal or spiritual, of any foreign prince, power or potentate"—at that time the pope was a foreign potentate—and sounding

the slogan, familiar in Chicago, "Our country, right
or wrong." The following year the party secured
complete control of the government of New York City,
electing as mayor James Harper of the publishing
house of Harper & Brothers. At the same time it
had complete or partial success in Boston, Philadelphia, St. Louis and New Orleans.

In Philadelphia the campaign was marked by a
violent episode known as "the Kensington Massacre,"
in which eight persons were killed and many more
wounded in an attempt to break up a political meeting which was being held by this party. It was reported that the riot was staged by the Irish. A few
days later a committee appointed by the sheriff forced
its way into the Catholic church on Queen Street, and
found concealed a considerable quantity of arms and
ammunition.

This is interesting because it may afford the original ground for all the wild stories that have been
subsequently circulated in regard to weapons stored
in Catholic churches and emplacements for artillery
being built into the foundations of Catholic schools
and convents on commanding hilltops overlooking
cities. The Philadelphia episode probably happened.
The contemporary evidence seems clear enough. But
if it did, it proves nothing but the bitterness of a
local political fight. There is another side to the
story, too. The Catholic Encyclopedia (article,

"Knownothingism"), omitting the episode here narrated, records anti-Catholic riots in Philadelphia and the burning of two churches.

The American Republican party also collapsed quite promptly after its initial rather surprising local victories. It probably owed that success, such as it was, largely to Whig support in local elections in exchange for promised votes for the Whig national candidates.

The next anti-Catholic movement was a secret order. Reflecting that secrecy was one secret of the strength of the Jesuits and that the Jesuits were the strength of Romanism, its promoters resolved to take a leaf from the enemy's book and be secret. The "Order of United Americans" was organized in New York, on Dec. 21, 1844. Its first activity was in connection with the New York public school fight, which was still going on in 1845, and its second in the campaign against the adoption of the new constitution of the state of New York, which eliminated the provisions that only native-born citizens should be eligible for the offices of governor and lieutenant-governor and that ministers of religion were ineligible to public office. The new constitution, however, was adopted.

The Order of United Americans grew rapidly and merged itself later in the Know Nothing movement, which, beginning also as a secret order in 1849, presently became a political party, standing between the Whigs and the Democrats. It attempted to crowd the slavery question into the background and to put into the foreground the questions of immigration, naturalization, public schools with the Bible not excluded, and "resistance to the aggressive policy and corrupting tendencies of the Roman Catholic Church." Under the official name of the "American Party," it had a tremendous success in the elections of 1855, chiefly by drawing to itself those who wished to hush up the slavery controversy—which was very much like trying to hush up Vesuvius—and maintain the status quo. Nation-wide and apparently flourishing in 1855, it virtually disappeared in 1856. Though professedly an anti-Catholic party, even its temporary success was no index of anti-Catholic sentiment, or even of anti-foreign prejudice.

Whether or not there was ground for the belief that the existence of a large mass of imperfectly assimilated immigrants, largely belonging to a church having its headquarters over-seas and claiming control through its hierarchy of all spiritual and all "mixed" matters, constituted or now constitutes a political menace, there has been an element of hysteria in all of these anti-Catholic organizations which has robbed them of any considerable influence upon thoughtful minds. Whatever may need to be done— if anything—to prevent the Roman Catholic church from exercising an undue influence in American politics, and especially in the determination of those "mixed" questions over which it undoubtedly claims jurisdiction but which the government of this country, under its present laws, reserves for civil control, it is historically demonstrated that the thing *not* to do is to organize a political party or a secret society. For further confirmation of the last item in this judgment, consider the tragi-comic futility of the American Protective Association, which rose and fell in the nineties, and of the Ku Klux Klan.

HAS THE IMMIGRANT KEPT THE FAITH?

Whether or not Catholicism is holding its own— that is to say, keeping the allegiance of the American-born children of Catholic immigrants—is a question that has been hotly debated among Catholics themselves. As early as 1836, Bishop England said that the Catholic church had lost three and three quarters million in the preceding fifty years. The "Lucerne Memorial" in 1891 put the loss up to that time at sixteen millions. By 1910, the author of that memorial, Mr. Cahensly, took a somewhat less gloomy view of the matter and presented to the pope another memorial putting the losses at ten million. The Abbè Villeneuve estimated in 1890 that there were twenty million fewer Catholics in the United States than there would have been if the immigrant had kept the faith and transmitted it to his descendants.

None of these estimates is reliable, least of all the last. More credence can be given to Gerald Shaughnessy's study ("Has the Immigrant Kept the

Faith," New York, 1925), which supports the view
that the Catholic population in 1920 was approximately what it ought to have been in view of the
number of communicants at the beginning of the nineteenth century, the number of immigrants, the percent of Catholics among the immigrants, the birth
and death rates, and the probable number of conversions. Many complicated factors enter into such a
statistical study, and I am not prepared to guarantee
even the approximate accuracy of his results, but after
considering his analysis of the facts in comparison
with the estimates which he criticizes, I incline to the
opinion that his is the most trustworthy of all the
estimates quoted. "It is absolutely certain that there
has been no enormous loss to the faith because of
immigration, and it is very probable that there has
been no loss at all, beyond that defection of Catholics which ordinarily takes place among any population."

The total number of converts in the century ending with 1920 he estimates at 883,000. Probably not
more than 300,000 of these are now living. The re-
mainder of the twenty million Catholics now in the
United States are immigrants, descendants of immigrants, and descendants of the original thirty thousand.

The numerical growth of the Catholic church and
its relation to the total population is indicated by the
following table of statistics, in which it should be
understood that the figures for the earlier period are
more or less conjectural:

Year	Catholic population	Total population	Catholic percent of total	Immigrants preceding decade
1790	30,000	3,929,000	.78	
1800		5,308,000		
1810	75,000	7,239,000	1.03	
1820	224,000	9,633,000	2.32	
1830	361,000	12,866,000	2.80	23,031
1840	1,000,000	17,069,000	5.85	212,479
1850	1,726,000	23,191,000	7.44	549,739
1860	3,000,000	31,443,000	9.65	1,114,564
1870	4,685,000	38,558,000	11.83	1,021,733
1880	7,067,000	50,155,000	14.09	1,276,990
1890	10,627,000	62,622,000	16.97	3,258,763
1900	12,041,000	76,303,000	15.78	3,794,112
1910	16,363,000	91,972,000	17.79	4,797,877
1920	19,828,000	105,710,000	18.76	5,735,811

It may surprise many readers to know that even a church with such strong central control has difficulty in getting an accurate count of its own members. The editors of the Catholic Directory complain of the lack of reports from many parishes and dioceses and the evident inaccuracy of others. They are, however, doubtless among the most accurate of religious statistics.

The "Catholic population" includes not only confirmed communicants but all members of Catholic families and all who, once Catholic, have never formally repudiated their connection with the church. It includes all who will probably become communicants if they live, and all who will probably call for a priest when they die.

The figures for immigration before 1830 are incomplete. Immigration must have been more, or Catholic growth less, 1820-1840, than the table indicates. The figure for Catholic population in 1840 is probably too high. Shaughnessy puts it under 700,000.

V

THE CATHOLIC UTOPIA

Would the Catholic church be intolerant today if it had the power? Would it change our form of government to the extent of giving to itself a favored position before the law? Would it take under its own control certain matters which are now subject to civil jurisdiction? In short, is it content with a legal equality with other religious organizations, or does it seek a status of legalized superiority over them?

These are questions which will test any man's capacity for clear and unprejudiced thinking. The evidence upon which the answers must rest will necessarily be drawn partly from the facts of history, and partly from utterances of those who are the official spokesmen for Catholicism. Partly also from the essential nature of Catholicism as revealed in its own statements.

Most Catholics and many Protestants who discuss the possible nomination or election of a Catholic to high political office—the presidency, for example—assert that the religious question is one that ought not to be raised in connection with eligibility to public office, and that to raise it is to be guilty of the grossly un-American crime of intolerance. As a general proposition, such a statement is sound. But in defense of those who think that this country ought not to have a Catholic president, it ought to be said that it is precisely because they believe in tolerance that, rightly or wrongly, they take this position. It is because they believe the Catholic church to be intolerant whenever it has the power to be so, that they think the reins of government ought not to be committed to Catholic hands.

There are reasonable, but debatable, limits to tolerance in several directions, but there is a limit in one direction which is so inherently necessary that it is scarcely debatable. Tolerance must stop short of tolerating a regime of intolerance. There are no two sides to such a proposition as that. Catholics will agree to it as readily as Protestants, though they will find different illustrations of intolerance. Some months ago the dean of a Jesuit university, speaking at a good will dinner to a company of Protestants and Jews, startled his auditors by declaring that he came to preach a gospel of intolerance—"an intolerance of intolerance," he added, amid great applause.

So the question at issue in regard to the wisdom and propriety of electing a Catholic President of the United States is not so much one of principle as one of fact. A person of tolerant mind is not estopped from taking the religion of a candidate into consideration if it involves his relation to an organization which he has reason to consider intolerant. He may arrive at wrong conclusions about the matter, but he has a right to consider it in the light of the evidence.

The relation of the Catholic church to the civil state has given occasion for more conflict and controversy than any other single item. Probably it will always be so, as long as the church and the state attempt to exercise concurrent jurisdiction over the same individuals. If the state would agree to give the force of law to whatever the church decrees, of course there would be no conflict. If the church would agree to exercise no authority in any field which the state claims the right to control, there would be no conflict. If there were in the nature of things a perfectly clear line of demarcation between the areas of civil and political interests on the one hand and moral and religious interests on the other, there would be no conflict.

CONFLICTING SOVEREIGNTIES

But none of these conditions is fulfilled. A non-Catholic state will not make itself merely the "secular arm" to do the bidding of the spiritual head. A church which claims to exercise authority at all cannot permit the civil state, made up largely of non-religious persons, to define the limits of its authority. And the boundary between religious and secular interests is not one which can be drawn clearly and sharply so that both sides will inevitably agree to it.

Probably the most nonsensical thing that sensible people permit themselves to say about the relation between church and state is that there can be no conflict between them because, though they have to do with the same people, they deal with different subject matter. Hear, for example, the words of Archbishop Ireland: "No room is there for discord or contradiction. Church and state cover separate and distinct zones of thought and action: the church busies itself with the spiritual, the state with the temporal. The church and the state are built for different purposes, the church for heaven, the state for earth. The line of demarcation between the two jurisdictions was traced by the unerring finger of Him who is the master of both. The law of God is—'render to Caesar the things that are Caesar's and to God the things that are God's.'" In similar vein Pope Leo XIII wrote: "God has divided the government of the human race between two principalities, the ecclesiastical and the civil; the one being set over the divine, the other over human things. Each is supreme in its own sphere; each has fixed limits within which it moves."

Bishop Spaulding some years ago, speaking of the Apostolic Delegate Satolli, said that "his authority is ecclesiastical merely and concerns Catholics not as citizens but as members of the church." And further: "Our obedience to the pope is confined to the domain of religious faith, morals, and discipline; and since the state claims no jurisdiction over such matters, there can be no question of conflict."

It requires, however, the most absurd ignorance of history, or the most reckless disregard of it, to assert the impossibility of such an overlapping of the areas of control claimed by church and state, and the

church has always asserted its right to define the
frontiers between the two.

We find Pius IX declaring, in the Syllabus of
Errors, in 1864, that it is an error to assert "that, in
case of conflicting laws between the two powers, the
civil law ought to prevail." The possibility of conflict is here clearly recognized, and that the authority
of the church is either equal or superior in the disputed area is as clearly asserted. Whether equal or
superior, in his view, was indicated clearly enough
when he declared the Italian Law of Guarantees of
1871 to be null and void, and when in 1875 he "abrogated and annulled" the Falk Laws of Germany.

Just how far a pope could go in the old days without *in his own judgment* encroaching upon the field of
politics, and by what arguments the defenders of the
papacy today support his views, is indicated by these
words which date no farther back than 1924: "When
a pope excommunicated a prince or king, the act was
clearly one of spiritual jurisdiction. When, as sometimes happened, it was followed by a papal declaration releasing the subjects of the excommunicated
person from their oaths of allegiance, the latter pronouncement was likewise of a spiritual nature; for
it directly concerned the binding obligation of an oath,
which is primarily a religious engagement. The question whether the subjects of a Christian prince who
had apostatized from the true faith were still obliged
to give him obedience, was obviously a question of
religion and morals. Unless we maintain that the state

is supreme in matters of morality and religion, we cannot concede it the right to decide such a question. Therefore, an authoritative decision could come only from the church. The effect of a decision unfavorable to the ruler was, indeed, quite the same as though the pope had claimed the right to depose him directly. The king lost his kingdom. Nevertheless the course of action followed by the pope was spiritual and moral throughout. At no point did it involve any claim of direct civil power." (John A. Ryan: "The State and the Church," page 44.)

So Catholics are still defending the kind of papal action which, though "spiritual and moral throughout," has just the same effect on the state as if it were temporal and political.

As a matter of history, the Roman Catholic church has always clashed with the state wherever and whenever the government has not been subservient to it. This may conceivably have been the fault of the state. But whosesoever fault it was, it has resulted from a chronic and apparently inevitable inability of the two to agree upon the limits of their respective areas of control. At the present moment I am not concerned to place the blame upon either party but merely to make it clear that this assertion of a natural and obvious distinction between the two fields of authority is mere words. Even if one were disposed to concede that rendering unto God the things that are God's necessarily means rendering implicit obedience to the Roman Catholic church in all matters of faith and morals, it still remains to be decided just what things are God's in this specific sense. And this is the point upon which there has never been agreement and upon which there is not likely to be agreement in a non-Catholic state.

What we actually find, then, is a church constantly claiming the right to control the actions of men in respect to certain matters over which the state also claims authority.

THE LAMENTABLE RAGE FOR EQUALITY

The most fundamental of these matters, so far as we are concerned, is the principle of popular government. Feeling the contradiction implicit in the existence side by side of a democratic government and an autocratic church, Leo XIII, in his encyclical of November 1, 1885, wrote:

"Sad it is to call to mind how the harmful and lamentable rage for innovation which rose to a climax in the sixteenth century threw first of all into confusion the Christian religion, and next by natural sequence invaded the precincts of philosophy, whence it spread amongst all classes of society. From this source, as from a fountain head, burst forth all those later tenets of unbridled license, which, in the midst of the terrible upheavals of the last century, were wildly conceived and boldly proclaimed as the principles and foundation of that new jurisprudence which was not merely previously unknown, but was at variance on many points with not only the Christian but even with the natural law.

"Among these principles the main one lays down that, as all men are alike by race and nature, so in like manner all are equal in the control of their life; that each one is so far his own master as to be in no sense under the rule of any other individual; that each is free to think on every subject just as he may choose and to do whatever he may like to do; that no man has any right to rule over other men. In a society grounded upon such maxims, all government is nothing more or less than the will of the people, and the people, being under the power of itself alone, is alone its own ruler. It does choose nevertheless some to whose charge it may commit itself, but in such wise that it makes over to them not the right so much as the business of governing, to be exercised, however, in its name."

No amount of interpretation can make out of this anything except a declaration that the head of the Catholic church regards popular government and political equality as false and dangerous principles. When he says that democracy teaches that "each is free to do whatever he may like to do," he is describing anarchy rather than democracy, but the defender of autocracy never can see much difference between the two; and when, in the same connection, he laments that "the authority of God is passed over in silence just as if there were no God," what he clearly has in mind is that the authority of the Roman Catholic church is passed over in silence just as though it were not the sole and infallible exponent of the will of God.

It is true that Archbishop Ireland says: "By the terms of the federal constitution, as by the teachings of the Catholic church, no room is given in America for discord between Catholicism and Americanism, between my Catholic faith and my civic and political allegiance."

But a pope is a higher authority than an archbishop.

It is also true that Leo XIII wrote: "The right of command is not in itself linked to any one form of government . . . There is no reason why the church should prefer one form of government to another, provided the form that is chosen be just in itself and favorable to the common good." The previous statement, however, makes it quite clear that to the pontifical mind a government in which "the people is its own ruler" is not one that is favorable to the common good.

The famous convert, Orestes A. Brownson, in his Quarterly Review in 1845—a period when the church was somewhat more outspoken about some things than it is now—wrote: "Democracy is a mischievous dream wherever the Catholic Church does not predominate to inspire the people with reverence and to teach and accustom them to obedience to authority." And again: "If the papacy is founded in divine right it is supreme over whatever is founded in human right, and then your institutions should be made to har-

monize with it, and not it with your institutions."
While there was some question as to Brownson's orthodoxy, the nearest he ever came to being repri-
manded was when Cardinal Franzelin advised him to
express his opinions with more moderation; but, on
the other hand, twenty-five bishops and archbishops—
nearly all there were in the United States at that
time—gave him, shortly after the publication of the
above statement, a signed endorsement which he carried for years on the cover of his Review.

It seems to be fairly established, then, that while
the Catholic church does not explicitly sanction any
one form of government to the exclusion of all others,
it is suspicious of democracy and considers it toler-
able only upon the condition that its individual citizens
are subject to the authority of the Roman Catholic
church and have been disciplined into obedience to
it in all matters which it considers within its field of
interest.

FREEDOM OF THOUGHT AN EVIL

The Catholic church is opposed to the separation
of church and state wherever and whenever it can gain
any advantage by the union of the two. Pius IX, in
the Syllabus of Errors issued in 1864, holds that it is
an error to say "that the church ought to be separated
from the state and the state from the church." Certainly it does not desire the union of the state with
a Protestant church, but it clings to the idea of the

union of the state with the Catholic church whenever this is possible, and it demands for the Catholic church both the special protection of the state and the right to exercise in its own name certain functions of temporal government.

Pius IX again: It is an error to assert "that ecclesiastical courts for temporal causes of the clergy, whether civil or criminal, ought to be abolished." The clergy then should not be amenable to the laws of the land or subject to its courts, even in criminal cases.

It is an error to assert "that the church has not the power of availing herself of force or any direct or indirect temporal power." This asserts the right of the church not only to be supported by the state but to exercise on her own behalf the power of a state.

It is an error to assert "that in the present day it is no longer expedient that the Catholic religion shall be held as the only religion of the state, to the exclusion of all other modes of worship." The supreme and infallible Catholic authority here unmistakably proclaims that all other forms of religion should be excluded from the state. How can they be excluded from the state except by the act of the state itself acting as the ally of the Catholic church?

Does anyone think that these quotations are too old to give a true picture of *modern* Catholicism? Sixty-four years is not much in the history of an institution which prides itself upon existing unchanged

through the centuries and upon making no concessions to the spirit of the age. But we need not go
even so far back. The encyclical on "The Christian
Constitution of States," issued by Pope Leo XIII in
1885, tells us all that we need to know. He has been
speaking of that "harmful and lamentable rage for
innovation" which led to the establishment of popular
government, and of the dire results which follow when
the populace assumes that the right to rule is within
itself without regard to the authority of God—as
voiced by the Catholic church. He continues:

"It is a part of this theory that all questions that
concern religion are to be referred to private judgment; that everyone is to be free to follow whatever
religion he prefers, or none at all if he disapproves
of all. From this the following consequences logically
flow: that the most unrestrained opinions may be
openly expressed as to the practice or omission of
divine worship; and that everyone has unbounded
license to think whatever he chooses and to publish
abroad whatever he thinks. Now when the state rests
on foundations like those named—and for the time
being they are greatly in favor—it readily appears
into what and how unrightful a position the Church
is driven. For when the management of public business is in harmony with doctrines of such a kind, the
Catholic religion is allowed a standing in civil society equal only, or inferior, to societies alien from
it; no regard is paid to the laws of the Church, and

she who, by the order and commission of Jesus Christ, has the duty of teaching all nations, finds herself forbidden to take any part in the instruction of the people."

Perhaps we may pause a moment here to reflect upon this lament of the pontiff that "the Catholic religion is allowed a standing in civil society equal only" to that of other churches. If words have meaning, this means that he claims for Catholicism a unique standing in the civil state and the right to teach not merely individuals (which nobody denies) but the state itself. It will not do to explain, as Catholic apologists do, that this applies only to "a completely Catholic state." Leo is explicitly talking about the kind of state in which the theory of democratic government prevails. There is not and never has been, a "completely Catholic state" in which that theory prevails, and by his own definition such a thing is impossible.

It is certainly not assuming too much for ourselves to say that, by the year 1885, the United States had become at least one of the most conspicuous illustrations of a nation whose theory of government he describes, with some caricature, to be sure, but with sufficient accuracy so that failure to recognize it is impossible. This thing would be no clearer if he had said in so many words: The government of the United States is wrong in allowing to Catholicism nothing more than legal equality with other forms of religion.

In his interesting discussion of Pope Leo's encyclical, Father Ryan, whom Gov. Smith quotes as one
of the ablest interpreters of Catholicism, freely admits
that the pope urges the necessity of cooperation between church and state and the specific recognition of
Catholicism as the state religion. He says: "It is a
thoroughly logical position. If the State is under
moral compulsion to profess and promote religion, it
is obviously obliged to profess and promote only the
religion that is true; for no state is justified in supporting error or in according to error the same recognition as to truth." (John A. Ryan and M. F. X.
Millar, S. J.: "The State and the Church," p. 32.)

A RECENT INTERPRETATION

But just what does Father Ryan understand as
being "essentially comprised in the union of Church
and State" which the pope so ardently urges? Father
Ryan is one of the most American of Catholics, a professor at the Catholic University of America, and the
leading spirit of the National Catholic Welfare Council, for which this book was written. He says: "The
principle of union between Church and State is not
necessarily dependent upon *any particular form of
union* that has actually been in operation . . .
All that is essentially comprised in the union of Church
and State can be thus formulated: The State should
officially recognize the Catholic religion as the religion
of the commonwealth; accordingly it should invite
the blessing and ceremonial participation of the Church

for certain important public functions, and delegate its officials to attend certain of the more important festival celebrations of the Church; it should recognize and sanction the laws of the Church; and it should protect the rights of the Church and the religious as well as the other rights of the Church's members.

"Does State recognition of the Catholic religion necessarily imply that no other religion should be tolerated? Much depends upon circumstances and much depends upon what is meant by toleration. Neither unbaptized persons nor those born into a non-Catholic sect should ever be coerced into the Catholic Church. Should such persons be permitted to practice their own forms of worship? *If these are carried on within the family, or in such an inconspicuous manner as to be an occasion neither of scandal nor perversion to the faithful,* they may be properly tolerated by the State. At least, this is the approved Catholic doctrine concerning the religious rites of the unbaptized. . . . Quite distinct from the performance of false religious worship and preaching to the members of the erring sect, is the propagation of the false doctrine among Catholics. This could become a source of injury, a positive menace, to the religious welfare of true believers. Against such an evil they have a right of protection by the Catholic State. . .

"Superficial champions of religious liberty will promptly and indignantly denounce the foregoing propositions as the essence of intolerance. They are intolerant, but not therefore unreasonable. Error has not the same rights as truth. Since the profession and practice of error are contrary to human welfare, how can error have rights? *How can the voluntary toleration of error be justified?* As we have already pointed out, the men who defend the principle of toleration for all varieties of religious opinion, assume either that all religions are equally true or that the true cannot be distinguished from the false. On no other ground is it logically possible to accept the theory of indiscriminate and universal toleration.

"To the objection that the foregoing argument can be turned against Catholics by a non-Catholic State, there are two replies. First, if such a State should prohibit Catholic worship or preaching on the plea that it was wrong and injurious to the community, the assumption would be false; therefore, the two cases are not parallel. Second, a Protestant State could not logically take such an attitude (although many of them did so in former centuries) because no Protestant sect claims to be infallible." ("The State and the Church," pages 34-37.)

"FIVE THOUSAND YEARS HENCE"

This is a long quotation, but it is much more interesting than anything that a non-Catholic could say about Catholic intolerance, and much more convincing. It does not need a word of comment or interpretation. I perfectly agree with Father Ryan that the logic of the position is inexorable, if the Catholic fundamentals are accepted—that the Catholic religion is the one infallibly true religion and that "its possession is the most important good in life for states as well as for individuals."

But fear not, says Father Ryan. "In practice, the foregoing propositions have full application only to the completely Catholic State." To be sure, all non-Catholic forms of religion are error and "error has no rights," but it may be inexpedient to put on the screws. Pope Leo again: "The Church, indeed, deems it unlawful to place the various forms of divine worship on the same footing as the true religion, but does not, on that account, condemn those rulers who, for the sake of securing some great good or of hindering some great evil, allow patiently custom or usage to be a kind of sanction for each kind of religion having its place in the State." Patience is a virtue which generally looks forward to the ultimate attainment of an end which cannot be gained immediately without paying too great a price. Variant religions may be endured, under certain circumstances —"patiently."

With the Catholic view of the relations which should exist between Church and State thus clearly expounded, it must be evident that there are only two safeguards against the Catholicizing of the state and the proscription of non-Catholics: impotence and expediency. Naturally, Catholics will propose no union of church and state where they obviously have not the power to carry it through. Hence their great en-

thusiasm for toleration—in Protestant states. But
even in Catholic states with a considerable non-Catholic minority, it may be inexpedient to deprive them of
the liberty to practice their religion publicly, though
no principle is recognized by which they are entitled
to that privilege.

"If religious freedom has been accepted and sworn
to as a fundamental law in the constitution," says
Father Pohle in the Catholic Encyclopedia, "the obligation to show this tolerance is binding in conscience." "But," comments Father Ryan very frankly,
"constitutions can be changed, and non-Catholic sects
may decline to such a point that the political proscription of them may become feasible and expedient."
And what protection is there against this eventuality?
Nothing, except that it is not likely to happen. "It
is true, indeed, that some zealots and bigots will continue to attack the Church because they fear that
some five thousand years hence the United States may
become overwhelmingly Catholic and may then re-
strict the freedom of non-Catholic denominations.
Nevertheless, we cannot yield up to the principles of
eternal and unchangeable truth in order to avoid the
enmity of such unreasonable persons." ("The State
and the Church," pages 38, 39.)

Zealots? Bigots? Unreasonable persons? Oh
yes. He is referring to those who, as he says, by
their own principles cannot be intolerant but who
like to have their own religious liberty grounded upon
something more solid than the fact that, for the pres-

ent, the "political proscription" of their faith is impractical or inexpedient.

A CATHOLIC UTOPIA

I am quite aware that the picture which has been presented thus far in this chapter is not in all respects one which liberal and patriotic American Catholics would endorse as a fair and complete representation of the attitude of the Catholic church toward the civil state. Neither do I consider it complete, though I cherish the hope that it will not be found unfair so far as it goes. If it is criticized, it will probably be on the ground that it does not sufficiently recognize the difference between the policy which the church outlines for a thoroughly Catholic state and the one which it desires to put into effect in the United States under present conditions. Some attention must therefore be paid to that important distinction.

Leo XIII in his great encyclical was describing an ideal Christian state. Such a state would be Catholic as a matter of course. It would not be a state in which the people made laws for themselves, but one in which there were rulers who had the right to govern and did not merely exercise the business of governing as the delegated representatives of the people. Nevertheless, in view of the statement that the church is not committed to any one form of government, it may be fairly assumed that he would not consider a republic as something that ought necessarily to be supplanted by a monarchy provided it had the right

sort of citizens. If the citizens were all, or almost
all, Catholics who acknowledged the authority of God,
voiced by the Roman Catholic church, as setting
bounds to their rights as citizens and to the powers
of the government, even a republic might be a legitimate form of government. He does not say that it
would be, but it is a possible inference and he may
be given the benefit of the doubt.

In such an ideal commonwealth, there would be
no separation of church and state. Catholicism would
be the religion of the state as well as of its people.
Dissentient minorities—we are assuming that they
would be very small minorities, otherwise it would not
be an ideal state—would not be allowed to practice
their own forms of worship publicly, or to propagate
their faith at all. Liberty of thought would, of course,
be limited by the requirement to believe what the
church believes, as is the case in the Catholic church
at present. Freedom of speech and of the press would
be permitted only to the extent of permitting such
utterances and publications as should not tend to the
spread of opinions contrary to those approved by the
church. Education would be paid for by the state
but controlled by the church. All matters pertaining to marriage would be regulated by the church.
The clergy, including both the regular clergy and the
"religious"—that is, members of the religious orders
—would not be subject to the civil courts, but would
be amenable only to church courts with reference to
both civil and criminal cases. The state would rec-

ognize the status of the pope as a temporal sovereign and would have diplomatic relations with the Vatican. The property of the Catholic church would be held by virtue of the inherent right of the church to hold property and not subject to any civil law. It would be free from taxation, unlike the property of such non-conforming minorities as might be permitted to own property. In short, it would be the business of the state to give effect to whatever the church might decree in the realm of faith and morals, or in respect to whatever matters the church declared to be in the realm of faith and morals, and to support and defend the church in the carrying out of such disciplinary measures as it might deem necessary to the success of its enterprise.

Now, quite obviously, this ambitious program is not one that could be put into effect in any country that did not have a vast majority in favor of it without precipitating civil war, and there is no ground for supposing that any person in the Catholic church, from the pope down, wants a civil war. Nervous Protestants may as well dismiss the fear that this system will be put over by a majority of fifty-one percent, or even by barely enough votes to amend the constitution, or by a coup d'etat of a Catholic president.

What are the hindrances to such a sweeping demolition of civil and religious liberty in the present and actual state? Clearly nothing at all in the principles which the popes have uttered and reiterated and have bound upon the consciences of the faithful with the force of immutable law and infallible truth. What then?

First, the constitution. "If religious freedom has been accepted and sworn to as a fundamental law in a constitution, the obligation to show this tolerance is binding in conscience." But, as Father Ryan reminds us, "constitutions can be changed." Also it is a principle clearly stated in the code of canon law that "the pope can release from every obligation, oath, or vow, either before or after being made." Still, the constitution, for the time being, is a barrier.

Second, the fact that the Catholic church has grown and flourished so greatly under a regime of tolerance and equal treatment of all denominations before the law that it will be slow to launch upon a premature attempt to secure a religious monopoly and proscribe all competitors. It may be intolerant in principle, but it is no fool.

Third, the temper and disposition of American Catholics. I do not mean merely the fact that Catholics love their country. If they agree with the popes whom I have quoted as to the constitution of the perfect Christian state, the more they love their country the more they must desire to see it conformed to this perfect pattern. Even the eminent American Catholic writers whose works I have cited show no repugnance to the picture of a country thus completely controlled by the church. They think that non-Catholics ought not to be alarmed, because the consummation is remote—perhaps "five thousand years hence"—but for their own part they contemplate that possibility with equanimity and approval not unmixed with hope, while they "continue to profess" the propositions of the popes as "the true principles of the relations between Church and State." Doubtless their love of their country quickens their desire to see it in the full enjoyment of that intimate alliance with the Catholic church which is essential to its highest welfare according to those principles. And yet the temper and disposition of American Catholics are a hindrance to the carrying out of any such program in its extreme form.

TRADITIONS OF LIBERTY

The Catholic citizens of America have grown up under a tradition of liberty and toleration. It is an American tradition, not a Catholic tradition. All the official utterances of their highest religious authorities are on the other side. But in the actual control of conduct and in the determination of social attitudes, the dictum of an infallible pope is no match for the forces of good will, neighborliness and the habit of friendly and tolerant cooperation. Few people are as bad as their theology, though fewer still are as good as their religion.

Imagine a Catholic president in the White House. Imagine a two-thirds Catholic majority in both houses of Congress and Catholic legislature in three-fourths of the states. Imagine the order to go forth from Rome to amend the constitution so as to abolish religious liberty and make Catholicism the religion of the state. (To the authority of the Roman pontiff "all are bound to submit not only in matters which belong to faith and morals, but also in those that appertain to the discipline and government of the church throughout the world"—and this would certainly come under that head.) They would not do it. I would trust Catholic voters, Catholic legislators and a Catholic president to refuse point-blank to put into effect the extreme doctrines which are embodied in the papal declarations as to church and state.

Why so? Because throughout history Catholic laymen have been rising in revolt against the efforts of the church to dominate the state. If Catholic France dis-established the church and freed the educational system from ecclesiastical control; if Catholic Austria abrogated the concordat of 1855 after the declaration of papal absolutism, declaring that this was not the kind of papacy that they thought they were dealing with; if Catholic Italy asserted its right to liberty and unity in 1870 and overthrew the reactionary papal government of Rome at the very moment when the dogma of infallibility was being pronounced —will Catholics who have lived all their lives under American institutions meekly vote to make the United States a dependent province of Rome? Never.

The bulls and briefs that have been cited are deeply significant. There is not a breath of consistency in the attempt to wave them away as documents dug up from "the limbo of defunct controversies"—

to quote Archbishop Dowling's phrase. The utterances of infallibility are never defunct, and even those deliverances of popes which are not certainly *ex cathedra,* and therefore not certainly infallible, are just as binding upon all Catholics as a matter of discipline as though they were. Nevertheless, most of the laity and the best of the clergy are more deeply committed to the ideals of tolerance than they are to the theory of what it takes to make a perfect Catholic state. Modern Catholics can not look each other in the face and deny the principles of religious liberty in the United States. Even an archbishop may—with utter inconsistency with reference to basic Catholic principles but a fine enthusiasm for American ideals—say, as Archbishop Ireland did: "Necessarily religious freedom is the basic life of America. Violate religious freedom against Catholics; our swords are at once unsheathed. Violate it in favor of Catholics, against non-Catholics; no less readily do they leap from the scabbard."

But if there is no danger that Catholics, if they had the power, would put an end to religious liberty in the United States and inaugurate a regime of proscription and persecution, is there danger that they would permit the church in any respect to encroach upon the domain of the civil government?

There is.

VI

AREAS OF CONFLICT

We have, let us assume, set our minds at rest as to the possibility of an immediate attack by Catholics upon the principles of religious toleration and the equality of religions before the law. We have seen that every recent pope who has spoken on the subject has denounced religious toleration and the equal treatment of different forms of religion; but we are assured that the principle, which the popes lay down and which enlightened American Catholics like Father Ryan elaborate and defend, for the establishment of the Catholic church as the one religion enjoying full legal rights, "has *complete and unconditional* application only to Catholic states."

It is not easy to find this limitation in the statements of the popes themselves. Leo XIII, in the encyclical of 1885, spoke with approval of the attitude of our government toward religion as having given a fine opportunity for Catholic growth, but added: "Yet, though all this is true, it would be very erroneous to draw the conclusion that in America is to be sought the type of the most desirable status of the church . . . The fact that Catholicism with you is in good condition, nay, is even enjoying a prosperous growth, is by all means to be attributed to the fecundity with

123

which God has endowed his church, in virtue of which, unless men or circumstances interfere, she spontaneously expands and propagates herself; but she would bring forth more abundant fruits if, in addition to liberty, she enjoyed the favor of the laws and the patronage of public authority." From which it would appear that he at least allows his imagination to play with the idea that, even in a state which is not "completely Catholic," there might conceivably be preferential treatment of the Catholic church, and that this would be a more desirable arrangement than the present governmental neutrality. And he does not seem to be contemplating a time as remote as Father Ryan's "some five thousand years hence."

PRESENT AREAS OF CONFLICT

But let us assume that the limitation which the pope's Catholic interpreters have stated holds good, and that neither the pope nor any American Catholic contemplates the granting of any special favors by the United States government to the Roman Catholic church this side of a very remote future. It remains to be considered whether the church proposes any encroachment upon our present field of civil government. If "complete and unconditional application" of Catholic principles is impractical in such a state as ours, then how much application is considered practical and desirable?

The plain fact is that the Catholic church steadfastly maintains its right to control, here and now, some areas which the state also claims. Quoting Ryan's summary of a paragraph of Leo's encyclical: "Under the pretense of separating church and state, governments have usurped control of marriage, confiscated church property, disregarded those rights over education which are inherent in both the family and the church, made their own determinations of the respective spheres of the two societies without consulting the church." Since it is evident that no completely Catholic state would ever do such things, manifestly the indictment must be directed against states which are not completely Catholic. (The State and the Church, p. 52.)

The supremacy of the state in the fields which the church considers her own constitutes what Martindale calls "Caesarism." "There has never been the time when the church did not have to oppose absolute Caesarism, whatever form Caesar took at the moment. . . . She has her own system and theory of just government."

Here are three definite fields of conflict between the Catholic and the non-Catholic ideas of the power and function of the state: marriage, property, and education.

MARRIAGE

The Catholic conception of marriage as a sacrament naturally and necessarily removes it from the control of the state and places it in the domain of the church. Where church and state are separated, surely the state has no right to control a sacrament. It has no right to determine who shall be admitted to a sacrament, or the conditions upon which it is valid or invalid, or to declare that it is null from the beginning, or to nullify and abrogate it. Which means that the state has no right whatever to make any laws concerning marriage or divorce other than to give its sanction and support to what the church has already determined with regard to these matters. Nothing could be much clearer than these words from Father Ryan: "According to the Catholic position, the State has no right to make laws affecting the validity of the marriages of baptized persons . . . She does not consider that human welfare, or social welfare, is promoted by State recognition of any marriage which she pronounces invalid, nor by State prohibition of any marriage that she declares to be valid." (State and Church, p. 50.)

Every Catholic, whether priest or layman, is bound to accept the authoritative teaching of the church on this as on all other matters of "faith and morals." And every Catholic, whether as citizen, legislator, or governmental executive, is under solemn obligation and strong social pressure to abstain from any act which would put into effect any practice at variance with what the church has determined about this subject.

The question at issue is not whether the position of the church is right or wrong with respect to the specific issue—say of birth-control, or divorce, or the requirement of a health certificate before marriage. The point is that, for Catholics, whether in private or in public life, these matters are already determined by the church—which means the hierarchy and, in the last analysis, by the pope as the supreme and infallible teacher of the church.

Unquestionably these are momentous issues. Public opinion upon them is in a state of flux. If they are to be decided upon a scientific basis, as an increasing number believe that they must be, perhaps we shall have to collect more information or even develop a new technique of research in social science before a decision can be reached. The plan of turning the whole matter over to the Catholic hierarchy for their determination may well be objected to by two classes of people: first, those who think that these are questions which must be studied and solved as social, not as theological, problems; and second, those who think that they are religious problems but that they should be settled, so far as this country is concerned, by the conscience and intelligence of the people and not by a small group of persons in some other country.

This last suggestion may seem like an unwarrantable intrusion of the nationalistic note in a matter that wholly transcends national boundaries. There is no nationalistic morality. If these are essentially questions of morals, and if all matters of morals are governed by revelation, and if the Catholic hierarchy is the only authentic agency for the transmission and interpretation of the relevation, the question of nationality is quite irrelevant. But that is only another way of saying that Catholics will naturally be quite satisfied to have American marriage laws made in Rome, but that non-Catholics may reasonably object without laying themselves open to a charge of bigotry, intolerance, or excessive nationalism.

PROPERTY RIGHTS

As to property, the United States has never confiscated church property, and it is to be hoped that it never will. But it is quite within the bounds of possibility that church property may be taxed by the states or that the income of religious corporations may be made subject to the federal income tax. The taxation of church property has been proposed more than once. Personally, I believe in it. Is a Catholic, whether as citizen, legislator, or executive, free to form his own opinions on these issues? He is not. His opinions are already made for him and authoritatively delivered to him by the church. The church holds that the right to possess property is inherent in the church. As a property-holding corporation, the church is not the creature of the state or in any way dependent upon the state. Therefore the taxation of church property would be an act of spoliation only less in degree than the complete confiscation of it, but not different in kind. The same would be true of a federal tax upon church income.

It is the collision of the government with this principle of the church's inherent right to hold property that has been at the bottom of most of the religious trouble in Mexico. It is not necessary to believe that the policy of the Mexican government in regard to property rights has been either wise or just. There are other corporations besides the Catholic church which are convinced that the Mexican government has not shown to their property rights the respect to which they were entitled, and many individuals have felt the same. But the church alone advances the claim that its right to hold property is inherent in its very nature as a divine institution over which the state cannot exercise any restraint whatever even with respect to the temporalities. Consequently, when the government declared that the title to all ecclesiastical property was vested in the state, the church denounced the law, obstructed its enforcement, and precipitated a condition which presents many of the phenomena of persecution.

The thing to note in this connection is that the church's protest against the act of confiscation did not rest upon a general theory of the inviolability of private property or of the injustice of the expropriation of the property of individuals or corporations, but upon the theory that the Catholic church enjoys a unique status as a body whose capacity to hold property is entirely independent of the law of the land.

The argument by which that theory is supported is perfectly simple and, to the Catholic, convincing.

The church is commissioned by God to do a certain spiritual work. That work cannot be done effectively without the possession of property. Therefore it is divinely commissioned to hold property.

But to claim such unconditional property rights is equivalent to claiming sovereignty as well as ownership. There is nothing that the church could conceivably do with or on its property which could not be defended against governmental interference by the same argument—that the act was necessary to the performance of its spiritual mission, of which, of course, it can allow no civil power to be the judge.

Property rights, therefore, constitute a field in which collision between the claims of the church and the policies of the state is perfectly possible and not improbable. In the United States such collision is not likely to arise in connection with any attempted confiscation of church property. If it did, public opinion without regard to sect or religion would leap to the defence of the church, not because we believe in the unique rights of the church but because we do not believe in the confiscation of anybody's property. But other issues, such as taxation, and the right of the government to such scrutiny as is necessary to determine whether persons are detained in convents against their will, may very easily arise. The attitude of the church on such issues is already fixed, and it is not an attitude which would be applicable only in a "completely Catholic state."

The school question is a third important field in which these are notable differences between the claims of the church and the position of the government and non-Catholic opinion generally. It is not merely a question of whether Catholics "believe in public schools." That is a trick question, like the one about believing in the union of church and state. It can be answered either way, and neither answer conveys any information unless further particulars are given.

THE SCHOOL QUESTION

Do Catholics believe that schools supported by public money ought to exist in the United States? Certainly they do. I have never heard a Catholic who denied it. Even the Syllabus of Errors makes no objection to public schools, in that sense, even in a "completely Catholic state"—if that is what the pope had in mind.

Do they believe that such a system of public schools should include in the curriculum religious instruction in accordance with the faith of the majority? Not unless that happens to be the Catholic faith. They believe that, in a Catholic country, the church— that is, the clergy—should have a hand in the direction of the public schools and that religious instruction, Catholic of course, should be included. In a non-Catholic country such as the United States, where any religious instruction that might be given in the public schools would certainly not be Catholic, they think that there should be none (except under a condition presently to be mentioned), and are quite uniformly opposed even to the reading of the Bible in the schools on the ground that the Protestant Bible is a sectarian book.

Do they believe in sending their own children to such public schools as have just been described? They do not. "It is false to say that the church has opposed the public schools in the United States. The church has never attacked the public schools. She has merely declared them unavailable for her children. For these she demands not only Catholic instruction, but a Catholic atmosphere in all the classes, both of which are out of the question in the public schools." (Rev. Joseph Husslein, S. J., in "God and Caesar.")

In the discussion of the Oregon school law—an ill advised attempt to require the attendance of all children at public schools—the Catholic argument made much of the inherent right of parents to control the education of their children. The accuracy, if not the sincerity, of this argument is open to question, for it does not appear that the church itself recognizes the parent's right in that regard. The new Code of Canon Law says: "Catholic children *must not* attend non-Catholic, neutral, or mixed schools; that is, such as are open to non-Catholics. It is for the bishop alone to decide, according to the instructions of the Apostolic See, in what circumstances and with what precautions attendance at such schools may be tolerated without danger of perversion to the pupils." (Canon 1374.) A Catholic bishop sums up the matter thus:

"Unless the bishop has given his permission, no Catholic may entrust his child to any but a Catholic school." (Bishop McQuaide, quoted in "America.")

Yet it is evident that, while the Catholic church does not attack the public schools, it carries its protest against the present system farther than merely refusing to patronize it. Granting that it would be impractical in a non-Catholic country to make all the schools Catholic which are supported by public money, why would it not be practical to give Catholic schools support by public taxation in proportion to the number of children who attend them?

The effort to get public money for the support of parochial schools dates back to the very beginning of the American public school system and connects with the system of tax-supported denominational schools which were in vogue until the 1830's. Protestant schools, as well as Catholic—and far more Protestant than Catholic—received government aid in the early years of the republic. It was largely the work of Horace Mann to discover that the constitutional principle of the separation of church and state required the separation of church control from the state-supported schools. Catholics, with their theory that a doctrine which is implicit in revelation may later become explicit in the teaching of the church and yet not be a new doctrine, ought to be the first to understand that this feature of the American school system, which required some decades to discover and put into practice, cannot therefore be condemned as an innovation. It was there all the while, implicit in the constitution.

As early as 1824 the division of public funds among denominational schools was discontinued in New York. Catholics did not long acquiesce in this arrangement. In 1840, Gov. William H. Seward, himself a Protestant—perhaps with an eye to the Catholic vote, or perhaps moved only by his own conviction as to what was wise and fair—said in his message to the legislature: "I do not hesitate to recommend the establishment of schools in which they (the children of Catholic immigrants) may be instructed by teachers speaking the same language with themselves and *professing the same faith*." The church threw itself with great gusto into the campaign on that issue, which amounted to a proposal to establish a system of foreign-language parochial schools under Catholic auspices but financially connected with the public school system. In 1841 Bishop Hughes, of New York, organized a Catholic party which nominated its own candidates for the legislature on the platform of "public money for the support of Catholic schools."

STATE SUPPORT FOR RELIGIOUS SCHOOLS

The same idea persists to the present day—that the church is justly entitled to a share of the public school funds for the support of its parochial schools. The experience of a century has convinced most non-Catholics that schools which receive public support should be subject to public control, that both the financing and the administration of schools is a function of government. The Catholic theory is that the administration of schools for Catholics should be in the hands of the church and the financial support of them should be a duty of the government. A recent statement will make this contrast clear: "Public schools are not an American institution in the sense that they are provided for in the Constitution, or that they were the schools prevalent in the country before 1830, or that even today they are adopted by all Americans, or that those who believe in them hold that non-religious education is an ideal system . . . In Horace Mann's mind, the only alternative was obligatory denominational schools and the present public schools. Catholics think that a third alternative are denominational schools for diverse denominations, such as Protestant England and Catholic Belgium provide for their various religionists." (McClorey, "The Church and the Republic," 1927, page 161.)

It was such a system of state-supported denominational schools that Archbishop Ireland had in mind when, addressing the National Educational Association at St. Paul in 1890, he said: "I would permeate the regular state school with the religion of the majority of the children of the land, be it as Protestant as Protestantism can be, and I would, as they do in England, pay for the secular instruction given in denominational schools according to results."

The American Federation of Catholic Societies, meeting at Buffalo in 1906, made this declaration of its position in regard to public schools: "First, let no public moneys be paid out for religious instruction in any school; secondly, let the educational per capita tax be disbursed for results in purely secular studies only in our Catholic schools, our teachers receiving their salaries as other teachers receive theirs; thirdly, to obtain these results let our schools be submitted to state or city examinations."

It is evident therefore, that the Catholic school question is still a live issue, and that the Catholic church is committed without any dissenting voice, so far as can be discovered, to the principle of demanding that a share of the public school funds be appropriated for the support of Catholic schools. It is sometimes specified that public money should not be used to pay for religious instruction, but that distinction is seen to be rather theoretical than practical when it is remembered that the church insists that the entire atmosphere of the parochial school shall be Catholic and that it shall not be merely a secular school with some religious instruction added to its curriculum.

The Pastoral Letter issued by the Third Plenary Council of Baltimore in 1861 said: "The only system that would be fair and equitable would be . . . if taxes are collected from all, to apportion the amount of these taxes fairly among the scholars taught certain branches up to a certain standard, no matter under what religious or other auspices . . . It would render the schools really *public* and *common*—which they certainly are not at present except in name."

But for a really clear cut and decisive statement of the Catholic idea about the public schools, the following words of J. A. Burns, President of Holy Cross College, in a work published in 1912, and especially his quotation from Brownson, leave almost nothing more to be said:

"In opposition to the view that responsibility for the education of the child pertains primarily to the state, the teaching of Catholics has been that the right and duty of educating belongs primarily to the parent; and, since education in the proper sense of the word is essentially a spiritual function, the control of the education of her own children rests ultimately with the church. This does not mean that the state has not the right to establish schools. But there is a great difference between establishing schools and educating, between erecting buildings, paying salaries and even compelling children to attend school, and the actual work of education. This distinction lies at the root of the Catholic view concerning the respective rights of church, parent and state in regard to the education of the child. The distinction has been clearly drawn by Dr. Brownson, one of the profoundest minds, perhaps, that America has produced:

" 'We deny, of course, as Catholics, the right of the civil government to educate, for education is a function of the spiritual society, as much as preaching and the administration of the sacraments; but we do not deny the state the right to establish and maintain schools. The state, if it chooses, may even endow religion or pay the ministers of religion a salary for their support; but its endowments of religion, when made, are made to God, are sacred and under the sole control and management of the spiritual authority, and the state has no further function in regard to them but to protect the spirituality in the free and full possession and enjoyment of them. We do not deny the same or an equal right in regard to schools and school-teachers. It may found and endow schools and pay teachers, but it cannot dictate or interfere with the education or discipline of the school . . . All education, as all life, should be religious, and all education divorced from religion is an evil and not a good . . . We deny the competency of the state to educate even for its own order, its right to establish purely secular schools from which all religion is excluded; . . . but we do not deny, we assert rather, its right to establish public schools under the internal control and management of the spiritual society, and to exact that a certain amount of secular instruction be given along with the religious education that society gives.' (Orestes A. Brownson, in "Brownson's Views," p. 64 sq.)

"Education being thus essentially a function of the spiritual society, its direction and control must rest ultimately with that society." (Burns: "Growth and Development of the Catholic School System in the United States," pages 222-224.)

GOV. SMITH'S RESOLUTION

Perhaps this is what Gov. Smith means when he says: "I believe in the public schools." Indeed, it is a perfectly fair presumption that this is what he does mean, for in the New York Constitutional Convention of 1915 he introduced a resolution, to quote his own words, "empowering the legislature to make an appropriation or to authorize a civil division of the state to make an appropriation in aid of denominational schools." (N. Y. State Constitutional Convention, Revised Record, vol. I, p. 375)

Another aspect of the school question which, to most observers, will perhaps seem to lie quite definitely outside of the field of faith and morals, is the matter of granting to the federal government a somewhat larger participation that it now has in the educational process. Yet the Catholic authorities align themselves quite unanimously against such a measure. I do not have access to any private correspondence that may pass among them or to any instructions which may be received from higher up on this subject. Perhaps there are none. But the unanimity seems too great to be the result of mere coincidence. Whatever the explanation, the Catholic consensus against the Sterling-Reed bill (formerly the Smith-Towner, then the Towner-Sterling) is so complete that one is justified in saying that the Catholic church is definitely committed to opposition to it. McClorey, in "The Republic and the Church," under a proper array of *imprimatur's* and *nihil obstat's,* denounces this as a measure which "would take the control of the public schools out of the hands of the individual states and place it in the hands of a newly created Secretary of Education at Washington," and lists the supporters of this measure along with such other enemies of state and individual rights, as conceived by the Catholic church, as the Ku Klux Klan, the prohibitionists, the Scottish Rite Masons, the socialists, and the advocates of compulsory arbitration in labor disputes.

The Catholic opposition to the federal education bill was largely in the hands of the National Catholic Welfare Council, whose executive secretary, Father Ryan, appeared before the Senate committee and said: "The National Catholic Welfare Council opposes the Sterling-Reed Bill." This organization is as much within its rights in opposing the measure as the National Educational Association, the American Federation of Labor, the General Federation of Women's Clubs, the League of Women Voters, the American Library Association, and a dozen other national organizations are in favoring it. The significant circumstance is the fact that the opposition represents the mobilization of Catholic strength against a governmental measure through an organization directed by a committee consisting of seven Catholic bishops.

The point I am trying to make clear is that there is a very considerable number of current issues of some importance upon which the Catholic church has taken a definite stand. These issues do not have to do with something that may happen "five thousand years hence," but with something that may happen next week or next year. They do not have reference to the possibility of setting up the inquisition, or making the pope president of the United States, or driving the Protestants into catacombs, but to the desire to impose upon the United States policies decided upon by Rome and in some cases specially favorable to the Catholic church.

OBEYING GOD RATHER THAN MAN

The difference between this Catholic pressure in the interest of the policies which the church approves and the pressure exerted, say, by the Methodist church in the interest of prohibition, is two-fold: first, they are policies which have been determined by a small hierarchical group and not by the common conscience of the total membership of the church; second, the Catholic church by its claim to a unique and divine authority exercises upon its lay members a degree of pressure which no Protestant church can exercise or tries to exercise upon its members. All those disarming generalities which assure us of the impossibility of conflict between the church and the state, because one operates in the spiritual and the other in the civil field, evaporate in the presence of such a frank statement as this: "In matters partly civil and partly spiritual, if church and state should have a difference, an arrangement could generally be made between them. But failing this, the spiritual must prevail over the temporal as far as Catholics are concerned." (McClorey: "The Republic and the Church," p. 163)

The danger implicit in this attitude cannot be fairly estimated unless the element of truth in it is also recognized. The Catholic says that if religious and civic duties should conflict, he would choose to obey God rather than man. But Protestants say that too, and have acted upon that principle repeatedly. The laws against dissenters in England in the seventeenth century were violated constantly for conscience's sake. The conventicle act and the five-mile act were considered iniquitous laws, and nonconformists by the hundreds went to jail for disobeying them. The Quakers, peaceable as they were, violated the laws regularly and suffered the penalties. Men of high moral sense will always do what they think is right in defiance of a law which they think is wrong. Abolitionists violated the fugitive slave law. Pacifists violated a conscription law. Placing obedience to God above obedience to man is no exclusively Catholic doctrine. Christianity would scarcely have gotten a start if men had not dared to do that. The voice of the state is not always the voice of God.

There can therefore be no just moral condemnation of Catholics if, in obedience to the authority which is for them the voice of God, they oppose a policy of the government, or seek in lawful ways to alter it, or, failing in that, refuse to obey it. But non-Catholics, who hear in the voice of the church only the utterance of a very human organization, will see in the resulting conflict

only the pitting of one human authority against another.   They will give Catholics full credit for the sincerity of their purpose to "obey God rather than man,"
but they will not on that account be required, either
by logic or by the spirit of tolerance, to aid and abet
them in making effective a program which Catholics
believe to be made in heaven but which others are sure
is made in Rome.

VII

A CANDIDATE ON THE WITNESS STAND

The open letter of Mr. Marshall to Gov. Alfred E. Smith and the reply of Gov. Smith to Mr. Marshall (Atlantic Monthly, March and April, 1927) brought some of these matters to a focus more sharply than any previous discussion of the relation of the Catholic church to the government of the United States and to the duties of citizens and officeholders in this country. At the risk of falling into the repulsive form of a syllabus, I will undertake to summarize Mr. Marshall's statements and questions and Gov. Smith's replies. The latter have a more than personal significance, since he explains that he enlisted expert assistance from Father Francis P. Duffy, who is well versed in canon law and Catholic theology.

1. *Mr. Marshall:* Catholic principles have been recognized as a potential obstacle to participation in politics. The encyclical of Leo XIII permitting such participation implied that there had been doubt as to its propriety. The Catholic church is committed by principle to intolerance. In asserting that God has divided the control of the human race between civil states and the Catholic church, it excludes any other church from any share in that control. The church, in the words of the pope, "regards dogmatic intolerance

as her sacred duty." Leo XIII said: "The Roman Catholic Church deems it unlawful to place the various forms of divine worship on the same footing as the true religion," but it does not condemn rulers who, for expediency, patiently allow "a kind of sanction" to other religions. Can such favors be accepted by free men in place of rights?

Gov. Smith: I believe in absolute freedom of conscience for all men and in equality for all churches, all sects, and all beliefs before the law as a matter of right and not as a matter of favor. "Dogmatic intolerance" means that the church does not tolerate variations of dogma within the church. Father Ryan, in "The State and the Church," has explained that the program of intolerance which the pope outlines has full application, in practice, only in completely Catholic states. Father Pohle says that "if religious freedom has been accepted and sworn to as a fundamental law in a constitution, the obligation to show this tolerance is binding on conscience." I stand squarely in support of the provisions of the constitution which guarantee religious freedom and equality. Archbishop Ireland said that the separation of church and state in America was a forward step. Archbishop Dowling says that the discussion about union of church and state belongs to "the limbo of defunct controversies."

2. *Mr. Marshall:* Who is to draw the line between the fields of jurisdiction of church and state? Every serious Catholic discussion of the subject admits that there is a middle area of mixed questions, partly civil

and partly religious. The Catholic Encyclopedia says that in cases of doubt or dispute, "the jurisdiction of the church must prevail and that of the state is excluded."

Gov. Smith: These are merely "speculations with which theorists have played for generations." The Catholic church has no tribunal or authority to decide such a question any more than any Protestant church has. Protestants have the same problem of rendering to Caesar the things that are Caesar's and to God the things that are God's. No member of the clergy has ever tried to influence me in a political matter. My cabinet contains 2 Catholics, 13 Protestants, and one Jew. In my public life I have exemplified the separation of church and state.

3. *Mr. Marshall:* The Church claims the right to control education and marriage. Do you approve?

Gov. Smith: No reply on this point.

4. *Mr. Marshall:* Leo XIII says: "It is not lawful for the state to hold in equal favor different kinds of religions." The Constitution of the United States holds the contrary. Which is right? Is our law of religious equality contrary to the will and fiat of God?

Gov. Smith: The previous explanation, that the principles laid down in the encyclical have full application only in a completely Catholic state, covers this point.

5. *Mr. Marshall:* In the case of the Oregon school law, it was not alleged that Catholic schools gave instruction contrary to the peace and safety of the state.

If it had been, the courts might have upheld the constitutionality of the law requiring all children to attend the public schools. If Catholic schools teach, as Catholic writers do, that in case of conflict the law of the church must prevail over that of the state, or that Protestants should be tolerated by favor, not by right, such teaching might easily be construed as contrary to the peace and safety of the state. What attitude should a Catholic take in executive office or on the bench if such an issue were presented?

Gov. Smith: It is unthinkable that any group of Catholics would teach that Protestants should be tolerated only as a matter of favor. I believe in the right of every parent to choose whether his child shall be educated in the public schools or in a religious school supported by those of his own faith.

6. *Mr. Marshall:* Pius IX says it is error to hold that "the sacrament of marriage is only something accessory to the (civil) contract and separate from it." The Marlborough case (reviewed at length) showed disregard for the sovereignty of the state in granting a declaration of nullity to those whom the state declared validly married, and upon evidence which would not have been taken seriously in any civil court in the world. Are such proceedings consistent with the peace and safety of the state?

Gov. Smith: The action of the rota no more attacks the sovereignty of the state than do the episcopal tribunals which refuse to admit the validity of divorce. The act of the rota has reference to the status of the parties only in the eyes of the church.

7. *Mr. Marshall:* In the Mexican church situation, Mr. W. D. Guthrie's brief, prepared at the request of the American hierarchy, protests that the provision of the Mexican constitution that "Mexican law recognizes no juridical personality in the religious institutions known as churches," violates international law, the principles of liberty and justice, American constitutional law, and the rights of the Roman Catholic church as "ecumenical and universal, founded for the governance of all men living under the skies." It quotes Lord Acton: "Where ecclesiastical authority is restricted, religious liberty is denied." Guthrie says: "Many historical precedents of action on the part of the government of the United States, as well as of other countries, could be cited which would abundantly support a protest or remonstrance, and even armed intervention at the present time in Mexico, in order to assure to the Mexican people religious liberty," and says that the papacy and the Mexican hierarchy refrain from asking intervention not because it is unlawful or unreasonable, but because of the dangers and horrors of such a conflict. Leo XIII wrote that Christ "commanded all nations to hear the voice of the church as if it were his own, threatening those who would not hear it with everlasting perdition." What authority do you attach to the voice of the church in this case?

Gov. Smith: The voice of the church, as expressed in the pastoral letter of the Catholic episcopate in the

United States, said: "What we have written is no
call on the faithful here or elsewhere to purely human
action." The suggestion of armed intervention has
been distinctly disclaimed. I recognize the right of
no church to ask armed intervention by this country
in the affairs of another merely for the defense of the
rights of a church.

8. *Mr. Marshall:* There is inevitable conflict in
the theory that the government of the world is divided
between two powers, a number of civil states on the
one hand and a church with centralized authority on
the other. Pius V deposed Queen Elizabeth and Roman Catholicism became synonymous with treason.
It took three centuries of gradual growth in toleration and good will to get the civil disabilities removed
from Catholics. And then, in 1886, Pope Leo XIII
beatified John Felton who, in 1570, contrary to the
law of treason at that time on the statute books of
England, posted on the walls of London the decree of
Pius V deposing the Queen. Granted that the decree
of deposition was a mediaeval episode representing
a mediaeval view of the authority of the pope over
civil states, still the beatification is almost a current
event and represents the modern attitude of the church
toward the state. And only recently the pope gratuitously insulted the Anglican clergy by telling them
that their orders were not valid. Is the record of the
Roman Catholic church in England consistent with the
peace and safety of the state?

Gov. Smith: The Pope did not volunteer his

opinion as to the validity of Anglican orders. The question was put to him and he answered it in the only way in which it could be answered consistently with the Catholic theory of the church. (No answer about the beatification of Felton or the deposition of Queen Elizabeth.)

A FEW COMMENTS

One wonders at the mental process by which Gov. Smith "knew instinctively" that Mr. Marshall's conclusions were wrong. Information counts for more than instinct in determining whether or not there is a conflict between two systems of government both claiming authority.

Gov. Smith was within his rights in calling in an expert adviser, but not in asserting that the questions which Mr. Marshall proposed were merely "theological questions." In so doing, he was apparently trying to wave them aside as merely theoretical and of no practical importance, knowing that the public which he was addressing had little patience with theology and little interest in it.

The patriotism of Father Duffy, attested by his war record, and of the "tens of thousands of young Catholics who have risked and sacrificed their lives in defence of their country," is not relevant to the issue. A man might have an excellent war record and an entirely wrong theory of government.

The denial of the possibility of conflict between the claims of church and state is too naïve. "No such conflict could exist." "If there were a conflict, I, of all men, could not have escaped it." But the possibility of such conflict is attested by every Catholic writer who has seriously discussed the subject, as many quotations in this chapter illustrate, and history has been full of such actual conflicts.

A moment's thought reveals the futility of seeking to sweep away the difficulties with such generalities as this: "The essence of my faith is built upon the commandments of God. The law of the land is built upon the commandments of God. There can be no conflict between them." The question is, what are the commandments of God and through what channels do they come to men? For a Catholic, the fundamental commandment of God is to obey the voice of the church upon all matters which it says relate to faith or morals and also upon those "mixed matters" which are partly civil and partly religious. The law of the land is not built upon that "commandment of God."

There is a spurious breadth in such a statement as "What we need is more religion for our young people, not less; and the way to get more religion is to stop bickering among our sects." What does he mean by "sects?" Is the Catholic Church a sect? Does he mean, as the statement implies, that the essentials of religion are something which Protestants and Catholics hold in common, that their differences are mere trivialities not worth spending time on? If he does, God bless him. He is not far from the Kingdom. But if he does, he is no Catholic. Where was his technical adviser when this appeal to American broad-mindedness was being penned? This is something very different from those references to "the true religion" which one can cull from almost any encyclical. Gov. Smith, having had his education in a parochial school, cannot know so little about the Catholic church as to suppose that it considers itself one of the "sects." His phrase has a generous sound, but it does not ring true.

Gov. Smith's apparently unequivocal statement of belief in "equality for all churches before the law as a matter of right and not as a matter of favor" is, in its surface meaning, so completely at variance with the words of Leo XIII and the explanation of those words by Father Ryan, that one is forced to look below the surface. When religious liberty has been guaranteed in a constitution and has been sworn to, then, as he reminds us, the obligation to grant that liberty is binding upon conscience. Or, looking at the matter from the other side, the individual would have a legal right to demand such liberty. So, for the time being, he enjoys it as a matter of right and not as a matter of favor. But that clearly does not touch the question that Mr. Marshall intended to ask. Everybody knows that, in a country which has embodied the principle of religious freedom in its constitution, citizens have a *legal* right to it. But what I suppose Mr. Marshall was trying to ask was whether the right to religious liberty rests solely upon these two fortuitous circumstances: first, that there happens to be a law on the statute books guaranteeing it; and second, that it happens to be inexpedient at the present time to inaugurate that regime of intolerance which Pope Leo and Father Ryan seem to agree would be the ideal thing in a Catholic state. What he wanted to know, I imagine, was whether Gov. Smith's devotion to religious toleration is anything like his devotion to prohibition, as something that should be enforced until and unless the law can be changed. The illustration is an exaggeration, I admit. I do not press it. But the answer, for all its apparent straightforwardness, does not touch the real question.

If Gov. Smith believes in "the right of every parent to choose whether his child shall be educated in the public schools or in a religious school supported by those of his own faith," he does not believe the Catholic teaching on this subject, which is that it is for the bishop or the ordinary to decide. There are many authoritative declarations to this effect besides the instructions sent out by the Congregation of the Propaganda at Rome in 1875 and the decree of the Third Plenary Council of Baltimore in 1884: "We not only exhort Catholic parents, we *command* them to send (their children) to the parochial school."

Gov. Smith says: "I believe in the public school." It has already been made sufficiently clear, in the preceding chapter, that such a statement means nothing at all unless one knows what kind of public school it is that the speaker believes in. Brownson and Burns believe in the public school "under the internal

management and control of the spiritual society."
They believe in public schools, supported by the state,
but "deny, of course, as Catholics, the right of the
civil government to educate." The Third Plenary
Council of Baltimore believed in public schools but
said that schools are not truly public unless the school
fund is apportioned among all schools, religious or
other, which come up to a certain academic standard,
The American Federation of Catholic Societies (1906)
believed in public schools, "our teachers (in Catholic
schools) receiving their salaries as other teachers receive theirs."

What kind of public schools does Gov. Smith believe in? An extract from the Revised Record of the
New York Constitutional Convention of 1915, vol. I,
page 375, will perhaps suggest the answer. It was
the session of June 10, 1915.

Mr. A. E. Smith: Mr. President, I offer the following proposed amendment.
The Secretary: By Mr. A. E. Smith. Proposed amendment
to the constitution.
Second reading: To amend Article IX of the Constitution in
relation to repealing section 4 thereof, relative to state and denominational schools.
The President: Referred to the Committee on Education unless
there is some other suggestion.
Mr. A. E. Smith: Mr. President, I don't know that I have
any objection, but the resolution is really empowering the Legislature to make an appropriation or to authorize a civil division of
the State to make an appropriation in aid of denominational
schools. It could very properly go to the Committee on Powers
and Duties of the Legislature.

There is nothing treasonable about such a proposal. It merely indicates that a man may say, with

all honesty, "I believe in the public schools," and yet believe in a very different sort of public school system from that which nearly everyone in this country, except the Catholics, believes in.

To make the record complete upon this point it should be stated, for what it may be worth, that Gov. Smith is reported to have said later that he introduced this resolution not with the expectation of having it passed but "as a bit of legislative tactics" to defeat another resolution which had been introduced abolishing the tax-exemption of churches and schools. The explanation does not seem to better the record noticeably. Since he introduced the resolution of his own initiative and not "by request," it is reasonable to suppose that it represents his view of the right policy with reference to public school funds, even if he did not expect it to be adopted. He could scarcely be unaware that his resolution stated exactly the historic and present attitude of his church. And as a "piece of legislative tactics" it could not be expected to have the effect of forcing the withdrawal of the obnoxious measure unless there was reason to suppose that an appreciable number of delegates would vote for it— presumably the other Catholic members of the convention. Taken simply at its face value, the resolution indicates that Gov. Smith favored the support of denominational schools by public funds. Considered as a "piece of legislative tactics" it suggests that he did not stand alone in that position.

Gov. Smith is far too indifferent to the utterances

of the Catholic authorities. "You have no more right to ask me to defend as part of my faith every statement coming from a prelate than I should have to ask you to accept as an article of your religious faith every statement of an Episcopal bishop, or of your political faith every statement of a President of the United States." This is literally true. But the "prelates" whom Mr. Marshall quoted were popes, and if the word "pope" is substituted for the word "prelate" in the foregoing statement, it is not true. The Catholic Encyclopedia is quoted as saying that the encyclicals are not "articles of faith," and Cardinal Newman as saying that the Syllabus of Errors has "no dogmatic force." This also is true, but in saying it in this connection he presumes upon his readers' ignorance of the fine distinctions of Catholic authority. A command of the church is binding upon conscience as a matter of discipline even though it may not be "an article of faith." The obligation of Catholics to accept the teaching of the church, and of the supreme teacher of the church, is not limited to the area for which infallibility is claimed, nor to the area of faith and dogma.

The Catholic press of Europe expressed surprise that Gov. Smith's casual attitude toward papal utterances should go unrebuked, and wondered whether some special dispensation had been granted. The Jesuit weekly, "America," warning the faithful against a general application of that seeming independence, said: "A papal encyclical invariably demands from Catholics, first, respect in view of the source from

which it emanates, and next, absolute obedience."
(Issue of April 30, 1927.)

Gov. Smith complains that his questioner seems to
believe that all Catholics think alike. Of course they
do not—about everything. But they are required to
think alike about all those things upon which an authoritative pronouncement has been made. At least
that is what Leo XIII says: "As regards opinion,
whatever the Roman pontiffs have hitherto taught, or
shall hereafter teach, *must be held* with a firm grasp
of mind and, so often as occasion requires, must be
openly professed. Especially with reference to the
so-called 'liberties' which are so highly coveted in these
days, all must stand by the judgment of the Apostolic
See and have the same mind."

Who is to blame if outsiders believe that, with
reference to matters upon which papal pronouncements have been made, Catholics all think alike?

To conclude this presentation of data regarding the
Catholic church and the civil state—the purpose of
which has not been to state conclusions but to furnish
facts upon which each reader can base his own conclusions—the question of the patriotism of Catholics
is not an issue. Only the most gullible and fanatical
can suppose that Catholics are plotting against their
country, or that they do not love it, or that they are
trying to tear it down in order to build the dominion
of the pope upon its ruins. There has never been,
so far as I can discover, one single incident or epi-

sode in American history which would furnish even
the shadow of a foundation for such a fantastic theory.

But if a man believes that the church is the one
channel through which the truth and the commandments of God are delivered to men, the more he loves
his country the more he will want that church to prevail in his country and its principles to be embodied in
its laws and customs. Sincere Catholics believe that the
Catholic way of life is the best, not only for the
church, but for the individual and for the country.
Innocent III did not want to dominate the Empire
because he hated the Empire, but because, among
other reasons, he thought that the Empire could never
be what it ought to be unless he dominated it.

The Catholic church is not to be blamed for trying to get what it wants, so long as it uses fair means.
The question is whether it wants what the rest of us
want. It is not unpatriotic in desiring to have its
way about education and marriage and property. It
considers its way the best for the state. But do we?

VIII

LEGENDS OF CATHOLIC TOLERATION

Two interesting episodes in early American history are often cited as proofs of the inherent tolerance of Catholicism. These are the founding of the Catholic colony of Maryland where, for the first time on American soil and practically the first time anywhere, religious liberty became an accomplished fact; and the alleged derivation of the principles of the Virginia Bill of Rights and the Declaration of Independence from the writings of the great Jesuit theologian, Cardinal Bellarmine. So much capital has been made of the first and such confident assertions have been made of the second, that they require some examination.

After the death of Queen Mary, Catholics in England had neither religious liberty at home nor liberty to seek liberty by emigrating to Catholic European countries. Shea's monumental "History of the Catholic Church in the United States," after recording briefly and colorlessly that Catholicism had been "restored for a brief term by Mary"—with no mention of any of those harsh measures in connection with that restoration which gave her the appellation of "bloody Mary"—proceeds to give all the gory details of the persecution of the Catholics under Elizabeth. They were quite sufficient to warrant horror at the present day, but the issue in Elizabeth's mind was personal and political rather than religious. She was prejudiced against Catholics because one pope's decision made her an illegitimate child and another deposed her from the throne and absolved her subjects from their allegiance. Shea explains that persecution on the ground that "Protestantism is essentially intolerant. Nowhere, on obtaining power, did it permit the Catholic portion of a nation to enjoy the exercise of religion even in private"—which is as true as a similar statement about the non-toleration of Protestants in Catholic states in the same period would have been.

Nevertheless, the three successive English sovereigns after Mary granted charters for the establishment of Catholic colonies. Elizabeth gave Sir Humphrey Gilbert a patent to lands on the coast of Maine, where the colony of Norumbega was established in 1583 under a charter which contained no limitation of the law-making power of the Catholic proprietor except that no law was to be made against the Church of England. Both Protestant and Catholic ministers were taken out and both sorts of worship were held, the former publicly for appearances and the latter privately. The history of this settlement was brief and tragic, and every schoolboy knows how Sir Humphrey's tiny vessel foundered in a storm on the return voyage.

Under a charter from James I, Sir Thomas Arundell sent out a colony of somewhat doubtful religious complexion in 1605. Its promoter certainly was a Catholic, and Shea thinks that the historian of the expedition, Rosier, was a priest who kept his record purposely noncommittal because "policy would require adapting the tone of his remarks to Protestant ears." At any rate, the proposed colonization scheme was abandoned on the advice of the Jesuit, Father Robert Persons, after the vessel, the "Archangel," had explored the coast north and south from Cape Cod and set up crosses at Boothbay Harbor and elsewhere.

But James, stout Protestant as he was—and therefore presumably "essentially intolerant"—did not exhaust his generosity upon Arundell. When George Calvert, a young man of noble family, educated at Oxford, knighted, and already a secretary of state, imperilled a promising political career by becoming a convert to Rome and resigned his offices, James kept him in the privy council, confirmed the title to his estates, exempted him from obligations which would have been odious or impossible to him as a Catholic, and created him Baron of Baltimore in Ireland.

Perhaps in anticipation of his change of faith, Calvert, now Lord Baltimore, had already bought the southeastern peninsula of Newfoundland from Sir William Vaughan and secured a charter for the colony of Avalon. "That it was his design to make it a refuge for oppressed Catholics cannot be doubted," says Shea. An extraordinary degree of autonomy was granted under this charter. There was no requirement of conformity to the religion established in England or of the enforcement of the English penal laws against

Catholics. The charter was granted in 1623, but when the colony went out four years later it found the soil and climate of Newfoundland unsuitable. Baltimore had, in fact, been among the first victims of a real estate swindle in western lands. He had long been a member of the Virginia Company, but the efforts which he now made to get a footing in Virginia for his settlers were frustrated by the opposition of the officers of that colony, who did not relish the idea of a Catholic invasion of their territory.

Meanwhile, Lord Baltimore died and was succeeded in his title by his son, Cecil Calvert, the second Lord Baltimore, to whom King Charles I granted, in 1632, an equally liberal charter for a territory north of the Potomac River. To quote Shea again: "A Catholic nobleman, at a time when his faith was proscribed in England and its ministers constantly butchered by law, was thus made proprietary of a colony in America where the colonists were to make their own laws, where no religion was established, where the laws required no royal assent. It was a colony where Catholicity might be planted and flourish."

CATHOLIC TOLERATION UNDER A PROTESTANT CHARTER

It derogates nothing that is due to the memory of Lord Baltimore, who was a large and liberal spirit, that quite as much credit seems to be due to the king for granting such a charter as to Baltimore for accepting it. If Catholicism was proscribed in England and "its ministers constantly butchered by law"—though as a matter of fact there had not been a priest executed in England for several years, so possibly "constantly" is rather too strong a word—it would have been folly for a Catholic to think of setting up, under the English flag and under a charter granted by the English king, a colony in which Catholics could with impunity persecute Protestants. Shuster, in "The Catholic Spirit in America," admits that "to some extent Lord Baltimore may have been governed by prudence in announcing his singularly liberal policy." To a very decisive extent, one must conclude, since he could not possibly have done anything else without bringing persecution upon his own head or forfeiting his charter.

The truth is that minorities are always in favor of toleration, whatever their principles. It is the possession of power to persecute that puts tolerance to the test. The Christians of the third century were all for toleration; they were in the power of a pagan government. The Christians of the fifth century, even such enlightened ones as Augustine, were for compulsory orthodoxy; the government was now on their side. Maryland was a Catholic colony, and tolerant; but it was a colony subject to the dominion of Protestant England.

And yet one need not quarrel with Shuster's further statement that Baltimore "and the men who followed him had been convinced by the trend of events in England that mutual forebearance alone promised peace and advancement in the domain of religion." If they had learned the lesson of tolerance as something more than a prudent policy for a minority, they had learned it in the school of persecution, with themselves as the victims, and not in the school of the Catholic church. There was not a Catholic country on earth at that time which practiced religious toleration, and not a Catholic theologian or ecclesiastic who had gone on record as favoring the practice of it toward non-Catholics. France, to be sure, was enjoying the comparative peace which followed the Edict of Nantes, but it was a peace of exhaustion and political expediency, which owed nothing to any Catholic advocacy of toleration and which was to be broken a generation later by the revocation of the edict and the renewal of the persecution of Protestants. Germany was engulfed in the horrors of the Thirty Years War, with its manifestations of utter intolerance on both sides.

In Spain, "in the sixteenth century the Inquisition had done its work so thoroughly that in the seventeenth there remained very little heresy to suppress" (Ogg: "Europe in the Seventeenth Century"), and according to the Spanish Catholic historian, Altamira, religion was as materialistic and pagan in its gross fetichism as it was intolerant of any failure in subservience to the hierarchy. Italy, the fountain-head of Romanism, showed not one glimmer of religious liberty in any of the dozen or more states into which it was divided. Spain, controlling the north and the south, could be depended upon to keep those areas free from it, and the Papal State never did make the slightest pretense of tolerating variations of religion until it passed from the control of the pope and was merged into United Italy in 1870. To say that Lord Baltimore's tolerance, such as it was, owed anything to his Catholic principles, is to strain credulity past the breaking point.

THE PROTESTANT MAJORITY IN MARYLAND

Unfortunately, Catholic colonists did not come to Maryland in sufficient numbers to insure the practical success of the enterprise. The original settlers consisted of twenty "gentlemen," all Catholics, and two hundred laborers, mostly Protestants. (O'Gorman says they were mostly Catholics, but the authorities seem to be against him.) Thus from the start the preponderance of Protestants in the colony put it beyond the power of the proprietor to proscribe Protestantism, whatever might have been his wish, since the charter, amazingly liberal as it was to him in other respects, gave to the colonists "the privilege of accepting or rejecting laws proposed by the proprietary." (F. R. Jones: "The Colonization of the Middle States and Maryland," p. 215.) In point of fact, the first draft of laws submitted by the proprietor was rejected in toto by the colonists for other reasons. How far would he have gotten in securing ratification of laws against Protestantism from this predominantly Protestant assembly?

But though Catholics did not come in the expected numbers, Protestants came in a stream which maintained and increased their majority. Some came directly from England; others from New England in response to an invitation from Calvert in 1643; others from Virginia. Lord Baltimore himself remained in England and exercised authority through his brother, Leonard Calvert, whom he appointed governor. After the death of Leonard Calvert, William Stone, a Protestant, was made governor, perhaps to remove the unjust suspicion that Maryland was a stronghold of popery where Protestants were persecuted. Under the new governor the *de facto* toleration which had been in operation for fifteen years was guaranteed by the Act of Toleration of 1649, which provided that no person believing in Jesus Christ should be "troubled, molested, or discountenanced for or in respect of his or her religion, nor in the free exercise thereof," imposed penalties upon any who should speak disrespectfully of the Virgin Mary, the apostles or the evangelists, or who should revile another on account of his religion, and made blasphemy against any Person of the Trinity punishable by death. Thus every form of Christian faith was tolerated, but blatant infidelity was not.

In brief, toleration in Maryland was the joint product of a non-resident Catholic proprietor holding title under a charter granted by a Protestant king, and an assembly representing colonists a majority of whom were Protestants.

What the early history of Maryland proves about any real or supposed Catholic tendency to toleration is exactly nothing.

THE BELLARMINE-JEFFERSON LEGEND

The interesting but unsubstantial legend which makes the writings of the great Jesuit theologian, Cardinal Bellarmine, who died in 1621, the source of the ideas of government which are embodied in the Virginia Bill of Rights and the Declaration of Independence, has gained wide acceptance among Catholics during the few years since it was put in circulation. It appears first in a paper by Mr. Gaillard Hunt on "Cardinal Bellarmine and the Virginia Bill of Rights," in the Catholic Historical Review, October, 1917. Mr. Hunt was chief of the division of documents in the Congressional Library. His theory has been reaffirmed by Dr. John C. Rager in the Catholic Historical Review, January, 1925, by Ryan and Millar in "The Church and the State" with amplifications and scholarly documentation, and by Cardinal Hayes in an address to the National Council of Catholic Men, at Detroit, October 18, 1927, as reported in the "Catholic News," October 22, 1927.

It has been demolished with devastating finality by Professor David S. Schaff in a paper entitled "The Bellarmine-Jefferson Legend" (in Papers of the American Society of Church History, Second Series, Vol. VIII, 1928).

The only ground for believing that Bellarmine's views could have afforded a starting point for the American theory of government is the fact that he opposed the doctrine of the divine right of kings. The particular king at whom this argument was aimed was James I of England. Pope Clement IX had, a little earlier, issued a bull commanding the Catholics of England to do all in their power to keep this Scottish Protestant heretic from coming to the throne of England. The denial of the divine right of kings was a useful item in the argument to prove the inferiority of the civil to the ecclesiastical power—which of course did come direct from God. It was an especially useful instrument against any particular king who happened to be a Protestant with Catholic subjects. How could even a heretical king be deposed by the pope if he had an independent divine right of his own?

The chief reasons for denying that Jefferson and the other founders of our government drew either their inspiration or their ideas from Bellarmine are that their ideas were radically different from his and that they probably knew nothing about Bellarmine's opinions.

The argument that Jefferson was familiar with Bellarmine's theory of government rests upon only two facts: (1) Jefferson owned a copy of Filmer's "Patriarcha," a book in praise of the divine right of kings, which contains two paragraphs summarizing, with a view to refuting, Bellarmine's doctrine that the power of kings was originally derived from the people; and (2) in a list of writers on "religious metaphysics" whose works Madison recommended to Jefferson as suitable for inclusion in the library of the University of Virginia, the name of Bellarmine occurs — along with one hundred and twenty-one others.

The chief points at which Bellarmine's theory of government differs from that which the fathers of our government adopted and incorporated into their declarations and subsequently into the constitution, are these:

1. Bellarmine considered monarchy the ideal form of government. He never for a moment contemplated the possibility of a government without a king.

2. He held that, while the power of government is originally derived from the people, when once the people have set up a king his power is absolute so far as they are concerned. The grant is irrevocable. Revolution, therefore—without special authority from the pope—is never allowable. The Virginia Bill of Rights, on the contrary, affirmed that, when a government ceases to perform the functions for which it was instituted, "a majority of the community hath an indubitable, inalienable and indefeasible right to reform, alter and abolish it." Bellarmine denied any such right, as Piux IX did in 1864 in his Syllabus. (It is not revolution, of course, to withdraw allegiance from a king who has been deposed by the pope.)

3. Bellarmine's plan of government has in it no place for representatives of the people. He specifically condemned the Geneva scheme of government because it included parliaments.

4. He bars religious toleration and favors the death penalty for heretics.

5.   Bellarmine does not even remotely suggest the separation of church and state and strongly implies their union.

6.   Bellarmine is quoted (by Dr. Rager) as saying: "All men are born free and equal." As a matter of fact, he does not say it. What he says is that "all men are born free." ("Omnes nascuntur liberi.") There is no hint of present equality. The implication of his entire system is that it is not every generation that is born free, but only the first generation in a country that does not yet have a king. Born free, they set over themselves a ruler and are free no more.

7.   While the separation of executive, legislative and judicial functions is as old as Aristotle, Bellarmine makes no mention of it. He is not even part of the channel by which that suggestion was transmitted to our times.

These divergences are far too wide to leave any excuse for such a statement as that of Cardinal Hayes that the "Virginia Bill of Rights was taken almost verbatim from the writings of the Venerable Robert Bellarmine," and that "the principles, almost the very language, of the Declaration of Independence were written by the Venerable Bellarmine."

It is true enough, as every student of history knows, that in the long struggle for civil rights the church and the people were often allies in a struggle against royal tyranny. But it was because they had a common enemy, not because they had common principles of free government. However complete may be the acceptance of the principles of the American government by American Catholics, they certainly did not learn those principles from mediaeval Catholic theology.

The legends of Catholic toleration in Maryland and of the Catholic origin of the Declaration of Independence will not stand scrutiny.

IX

PROMOTION AND PROPAGANDA

Considered simply as an organization, the Roman Catholic Church is the most elaborate and impressive social structure in the world. One has but to thumb through the thousand pages of the *Annuaire Pontifical Catholique* to get an almost overwhelming sense of the reach and sweep of it, its intricate ramifications, the complete co-ordination of parts, the world-wide scope of its agencies, the multitudinous personnel by which its activities are carried on, and the more than regal dignity with which it clothes the bearers of what it believes to be its more than human authority.

It has not only a wider territorial extent but a longer continuous history than any other existing organization. Its present total structure is the product of a long development, but many of its features are of comparatively recent origin—that is, within the last three or four centuries. The greater part of the administrative departments, the civil functionaries and the bureaux of all governments date back no farther than that.

THE CENTRAL ORGANIZATION

The central organization at Rome includes twelve Congregations, three Tribunals, and five Offices, all of which together constitute the Curia. The Congregations are standing commissions of cardinals. The most important are the Congregation of the Holy Office, which has control of all matters concerning faith and morals, the extirpation of heresy, the index of prohibited books, and, in general, the defence of the purity of the faith, and which formerly had charge of the inquisition; and the Congregation of the Propagation of the Faith, which controls all missionary activities. Of the Tribunals, the one that we hear most about is the Rota, which, among other things, decides matrimonial questions. The principal Offices are the Chancery, the Datary, and the Apostolic Camera.

The College of Cardinals consists, theoretically, of seventy members, but the actual number is always less. While they are all bishops, though many of them hold the title for sees that are no longer in existence (titular bishops), they are ranked as cardinal bishops (six), cardinal priests (fifty), and cardinal deacons (fourteen). This arrangement, so far as the cardinal priests and cardinal deacons are concerned, relates to their assignment as honorary priests of Roman churches and as members of the diaconate of Rome. Cardinal Mundelein, for example, is titular priest of the church of Santa Maria del Popolo. The cardinal bishops are bishops of sees in the immediate vicinity of Rome. Thus the entire College of Cardinals constitutes, in theory, the higher clergy of the city of Rome and its suburbs.

There is thus some logical consistency in conferring upon them the responsibility of electing the Bishop of Rome—the Pope. The College of Cardinals has exercised this important function since the twelfth century. As a group, they have no administrative or legislative function, but individually they are members of the administrative bodies that have been mentioned. Thirty-two cardinals are permanent residents of Rome. Of the cardinals listed in the *Annuaire* for 1926, thirty-six are Italians, seven are French, five are Spanish. Germany and the United States have four each. Ten other countries have one or two each. So the College of Cardinals is an international body with an Italian majority.

The choice of a new pope is made not only by the cardinals but, almost without exception, from their own number, generally one well advanced in years. The official list of popes, beginning with the Apostle Peter and omitting anti-popes during the schism, contains 266 names, so that the average length of a pontificate has been about seven years. Most of the early popes have been canonized, but none since Pius V (who died 1572), and none has been beatified since Urban V (died 1370).

THE DIPLOMATIC SERVICE

The papal Secretary of State is the head of the Vatican diplomatic service, and is thus directly in charge of the relations of the papacy with the various secular governments. The thirty-four governments which maintain diplomatic representatives at the Vatican and officially receive papal ambassadors include virtually all the important countries of the world except the United States, Italy, Russia, China and Japan. With many countries the Vatican has "concordats," which are in the nature of treaties defining the status and prerogatives of the church and in many cases assuring it a preferred position in comparison with other religious organizations.

The existence of these diplomatic connections is an evidence that the church considers that its legitimate strategy includes the exercise of influence directly upon governments. It is not disputed that the business of these papal ambassadors is to look after the interests of the church in so far as they may be affected by governmental acts and attitudes. This does not mean that the church is merely desirous of getting equal treatment. It gets preferential treatment wherever possible. For example, the Jesuit weekly, "America," speaking of the services by which the present pope earned his elevation, says: "To his untiring efforts (as nuncio) it was chiefly due that two articles were written into the constitution of the (Polish) Republic, namely: one declaring that the Catholic religion occupies the first place in the Polish state, and the other in virtue of which no measures can be taken by the State concerning the Catholic church without preliminary agreement with the Holy See."

A papal legate is an ecclesiastic appointed by the pope "to go to distant places where he cannot go and to take his place and exercise such jurisdiction as he himself, if present, would exercise." (Pius, VI, in 1789, replying to four German archbishops who denied the pope's right to send legates without the consent of the government into whose territory they were sent.) An ambassador, of course, cannot be sent to a government unless the government is willing to receive him. A legate differs from an ambassador in that he is sent to the church rather than to the government. There is a special excommunication against those who harm, expel, or unlawfully detain legates or nuncios. The term "nuncio" was introduced in the thirteenth century.

The Congress of Vienna, in 1815, made the nuncios the deans of the diplomatic corps at the several courts to which they were accredited, thus giving them precedence over all ambassadors of secular states. Later England and Sweden objected to allowing this honor to papal representatives of lower grade—for example, to apostolic delegates and internuncios—but it is generally granted, to this day.

Apostolic Delegates are sent either by the Congregation of the Propaganda to missionary countries, or by the papal Secretary of State to the church in countries which do not have diplomatic relations with the Vatican. The Apostolic Delegate to the United States thus has a purely ecclesiastical and not a diplomatic character. Any precedence that may be allowed to him is merely a matter of courtesy. The legation to the United States, however, almost equals in dignity a nunciature of the first class—which means that the incumbent is entitled to a cardinal's hat on his return from his mission. It was established by Leo XIII in 1893.

CATHOLIC MISSIONS

The strictly missionary work of the church is in charge of the Congregation of the Propaganda of the Faith. Under the direction of this Congregation, the Vatican Mission Exposition was held in the Vatican gardens at Rome in 1925. This was probably the most elaborate exhibition of the fields and work of foreign missions that has ever been given. Turning back into history, it portrayed the achievements and sufferings of the missionaries of the faith from the earliest days, and coming down to our own times it exhibited with great fullness the forces and equipment of present Catholic missions and the peoples among whom they work. The great Catholic mission fields are eight: North America (Indians, Eskimos and Negroes), South America, Africa, India, Indo-China, the Pacific Islands, Japan, and China. In the missions of these fields there are about 13,000,000 Catholics, of whom over 2,000,000 are in China, nearly 3,000,000 in India, and almost as many in Africa. These missions are manned by 8,632 foreign and 4,015 native priests; 3,183 foreign and 832 native Brothers; 12,933 foreign and 11,157 native Sisters; and 65,641 catechists or lay helpers. These operate in 66,352 stations, maintain 22,362 schools, 1,363 orphanages, 587 hospitals and 1,786 dispensaries, and operate 128 mission presses. These statistics are from "The Vatican Mission Exposition," by Rev. John J. Considine of the Maryknoll mission in China under the Catholic Foreign Mission Society of America.

ORGANIZATION IN THE UNITED STATES

The Catholic hierarchy in the United States consists of 99 bishops and 17 archbishops, four of whom are cardinals. Being a cardinal adds nothing to a bishop's authority either in his own diocese or elsewhere, though it adds greatly to his prestige and influence. For ecclesiastical administration, the country is divided into 14 provinces, and these into 114 dioceses and archdioceses.

According to the Catholic Directory for 1927, there are in the United States 24,990 priests, of whom 18,-111 are "secular" clergy (regular priests) and 6,879 "religious" (members of religious orders). There are several times that many religious who are not priests. Of the 17,651 churches, 11,823 have resident priests.

The chief administrative officer of each diocese is the bishop, whose seat is the cathedral and who may be assisted either by a "chapter of canons," or by a body of "consultants" chosen from the diocesan clergy, or, in case of very large dioceses, by an auxiliary bishop. Next in rank below the bishop is the vicar general who acts for him in many matters of administration. The diocesan chancery, headed by the chancellor, has charge of the correspondence and records. The diocesan synod, which is summoned annually by the bishop and includes some parish priests together with other clergy of higher rank, is a consultant, not a legislative body. "The bishop alone possesses all legislative power." The only layman in the organization is the "administrator"—who may be, but is not necessarily a layman—whose function is the care of the property, especially with reference to legal questions that may be involved.

Each parish, according to canon law, has perfectly definite boundaries, and is presided over by a priest who is ordinarily appointed by the bishop but cannot be summarily removed by him, and possesses a landed endowment to guarantee it an adequate income. The parishes in the United States are not strictly canonical parishes, owing to the fact that Catholics constitute only a fraction of their population and that few of them have the necessary endowment. They are "quasi-parishes" and their priests are "quasi-parish priests." Their boundaries are less exact, and the bishop has more power over them, both in creating and dividing parishes and in removing priests. Under canon law, every parish is required to have one irremovable priest, but under the plan in operation in the United States the proportion of irremovable priests is about one in ten. All are required to subscribe to the anti-modernist oath, in accordance with the decree of Pius X, Sept. 1, 1910. The parish priest administers the parochial property, and is held to a strict account for furnishings, equipment and collections, for which he must make a periodical accounting to the bishop. He is often assisted in the handling of property and finances by lay trustees, but no expenditure over $300, except for regular expenses, can be made by the priest or trustees without the written consent of the bishop.

Thus the diocesan administration of the church in the United States, far from being more democratic, is more completely centralized in the hands of the bishop than elsewhere.

In the early part of the nineteenth century the holding of church property in the name of trustees was the common practice with Catholic churches, as it is still with Protestant churches. Not without some controversy, this plan was abandoned in favor of having all property held by the bishop of the diocese. The exact legal situation in a typical diocese is set forth in an advertisement (April 1928) which offers for sale the notes for $1,500,000 issued by the Archbishop of Chicago, the proceeds of which were presented to the pope for the construction of new buildings for the Pontifical Urban College for Foreign Catholic Missions in Rome. "These notes will be signed personally by the Cardinal Archbishop of Chicago and will, in the opinion of counsel, constitute a direct, valid and binding obligation of the Catholic Bishop of Chicago, a corporation sole created by and existing under a special act of the General Assembly of Illinois, approved and in force, Feb. 20, 1861. A corporation sole consists of one person only, and his successors in office, who are incorporated by law to give them legal capacities and advantages not possessed by natural persons. Property rights, liabilities and certain other rights attaching to the office pass to the successor in office and not to the decedent's heirs. Appointment of the Archbishop of Chicago carries with it the office of the Catholic Bishop of Chicago. The Archdiocese of Chicago includes all of Cook, Lake, Du Page, Kankakee, Will and Grundy counties in the State of Illinois, the Catholic population of which is nearly 1,-500,000. There are over 360 churches in the archdiocese, and upwards of 200,000 boys and girls receiving their education in its parochial schools. Title to all the property of the Catholic church in the diocese, except some few institutions and parishes in charge of religious orders of the clergy, is in the Catholic Bishop of Chicago."

THE CHEAPEST ARMY IN THE WORLD

The religious orders are an immensely important factor in the ecclesiastical organization. Sixty-nine orders for men and 180 orders for women are represented. Of the men's orders, some, such as the Alexian Brothers, the Augustinians, and the Benedictines, are devoted largely to nursing; others, including the Brothers of the Christian Schools and most of the Jesuits, to teaching; still others, such as the Dominicans and Franciscans, largely to conducting missions and retreats.

The Jesuit order is itself a large subject about

which no person can possibly say anything without being accused of prejudice one way or the other. There are 3,637 Jesuits in the United States, 1,585 of whom are "fathers" (priests), 1,612 "scholastics," and 434 lay brothers. The Society of Jesus has aroused deeper loyalty in its members, more bitter hostility in its enemies, and blacker suspicion in other religious orders than any other organization in the Catholic church. It would not be fair even to enumerate the charges that have been made against it, when there is not room for any discussion of them. The record of the order for interference in politics was so bad that it has at various times been expelled from various Catholic countries; and this feature of its policy and its chronic quarrels with other orders were the chief grounds for the dissolution and abolition of the order by the bull of Pope Clement XIV in 1773. It maintained a more or less surreptitious existence until its restoration by Pius VII in 1815. But as an off-set to these two charges, it should be said that there is no evidence that the Jesuits have ever taken any improper part in American politics—unless the attitude of the church with reference to such matters as school legislation is considered improper—and that their relation to other orders and to the church as a whole in the United States, so far as can be discovered from the outside, has been generally cordial and cooperative.

I will evade responsibility for expressing any opinion upon the Society of Jesus by referring to three recent books, which present entirely different views. "The Jesuits in Modern Times," by John LaFarge, S. J. (The American Press, 1928), represents the order as without spot or blemish. The utmost concession is that "tactlessness, imprudence or vanity on the part of individual Jesuits at various epochs" may be alleged. Why then so much opposition? From the world because—"The servant is not greater than his master. If they have persecuted Me, they will also persecute you." From well meaning men within the church because of the apostolic zeal of the Jesuits, "rousing good men from too much sense of security, disturbing them by unwelcome warnings, and urging others to action who would prefer to be left at rest." "The Jesuit Enigma," by E. Boyd Barrett (Boni & Liveright, 1927) an ex-Jesuit who is still a Catholic, pictures the society as the church's worst enemy, a teaching body whose scholarship is pretense and whose methods are unpedagogical, a trap into which novices are lured under false representations and from which escape is all but impossible, a machine which crushes personality by discipline, compulsory uniformity and routine, and an autocratic society which tyrannizes over the church as much as it does over its own members. "The Jesuits, An Historical Study," by H. Boehmer (English translation, Castle Press, 1928), treating of the order only until its suppression in 1773, clears it of the more serious charges which were brought against it by Pascal and its other seventeenth century critics but finds it too much devoted to building up its own power and permanently committed to "the mediaeval idea of an ecclesiastically directed and controlled culture," and credits it—if it be a credit—with stamping its own pattern upon the modern Catholic church.

The religious orders for women are numerous and their membership is immense. I added the figures given in the Catholic Directory up to about fifty thousand, and then stopped, wondering whether there was something the matter with the statistics. But probably there is not. When one considers that there are more than a thousand Catholic hospitals, orphanages and homes for the aged, chiefly "manned" by women of the religious orders, and over seven hundred academies for girls, the personnel of which is entirely drawn from these orders, and parochial schools in seven thousand parishes with more than two million pupils, nearly all taught by "religious"—the number does not seem unreasonable. It must, in reality, be much larger. Of completely cloistered nuns there are very few.

The monastic life, at present, is as far removed from devout indolence and pious contemplation as one could well imagine. The orders furnish the private soldiers in the army of the church, the mass of laborers for doing its educational and benevolent work. Serving without pay, subject to the rigid control of their superiors, bound by irrevocable vows which make it impossible for them to withdraw without the utmost difficulty, and almost totally cut off from all normal domestic relations and from all social ties apart from their orders and their work, they constitute a wonderfully disciplined and inexpensive force for carrying on the enterprises of the church. Without them, it is not too much to say that the whole program, so far as schools and other institutions are concerned, would be impossible.

CATHOLIC SCHOOLS

There is no part of its total program of activities to which the Catholic church attaches more importance than to its schools. It has been so since the early days of the republic. There was at first no differentiation between public schools and church schools. As an early apostle of education, Father Richard of Detroit is worthy of memory and honor. He was, by the way, the only Catholic priest who was ever a member of Congress; that was in 1823. Before 1802 he had established an elementary school and a high school in Detroit, using French text-books. The act establishing the "Catholepistemiad, or University of Michigania" in 1817, is credited to him. It had an ambitious program—a complete system of primary, secondary and higher schools throughout the state, including "colleges, academies, schools, libraries, museums, athenaeums, botanic gardens, laboratories, and other useful literary and scientific institutions," all under the jurisdiction of the university and all to be supported by the state. Rev. John Monteith, a Presbyterian minister of Detroit, was president, Father Richard was vice-president, and they divided between them the thirteen professorships—at an annual salary of $12.50 per professorship. Meanwhile Father Richard's Catholic schools in Detroit were still supported by taxation.

In the east, the absence of any real system of public schools made the establishment of church schools imperative. The First Provincial Council of Baltimore, in 1829, urged it. The first "common school" in Baltimore was started by Father Moranville in connection with his church. Many Catholic schools were founded between 1810 and 1830. The devoted work of "Mother" Seton and his Sisters of Charity, and of the Sisters of Loretto and Sisters of St. Dominic before 1840 was notable. The Lowell plan, in 1831, gave to Catholic schools in that city and elsewhere in Massachusetts state support such as many Protestant schools were receiving. Throughout the middle west also the Catholics did their share in building schools and in many cases the teacher, who was sometimes the local priest, was paid from public funds.

In the 1830's a change in public sentiment occurred. It was due partly to immigration and the break of such religious homogeneity as there had been, and partly to the work of Horace Mann in establishing a system of public education independent of the churches. The "great school controversy" became acute about 1840. The Catholics, especially in New York, under the leadership of Bishop Hughes, fought the new public school idea by every means within

their power. They failed, except to the extent of securing the exclusion of the Bible from the public
schools there and in many other states, insisting that
if the state schools were going to be secular they should
be completely secular. Other influences, of course,
supported them in this argument.

From this, as a turning point, began the intensive
development of the Catholic parochial schools, with
no further concerted political effort to get state
support for them, but with constantly repeated statements of their right to it. An essential thing to remember is that the plan of giving state support to
denominational schools is not one which the Catholics
originated, but one to which they clung after the rest
of the country abandoned it.

Local compromises from time to time secured some
approximation to what the Catholics desired, as in the
Poughkeepsie plan which was in operation from 1873
to 1891, and the Faribault (Minn.) plan, fostered by
Archbishop Ireland, which was put into effect in 1891
and lasted in that place only two years, though longer
in a few other places in Minnesota, where Catholics
were in a great majority. These plans failed, partly
because non-Catholic sentiment disapproved of them,
but even more because the higher Catholic authorities
were suspicious of them as conceding too much to the
state. To make Catholic schools a part of a state
school system seemed to be an admission that the
state had a right to have a school system.

This Catholic attitude was perhaps best exhibited

in the "Bouquillon controversy," which began with the publication, in 1891, of a pamphlet entitled, "Education—to Whom Does It Belong?" by Father Bouquillon, professor of moral theology in the Catholic University at Washington. This writer argued that education is not solely the prerogative of the church; that the state also has a right to educate its citizens because it has a right to use all the legitimate temporal means it judges necessary for the temporal common welfare; that the state has a right to set minimum requirements for all schools and to inspect all schools as to hygiene and public morals, though not to require parents to send their children to a particular school.

TO WHOM DOES EDUCATION BELONG?

To most Americans these points do not seem doubtful or disputatious. They are merely corollaries of the proposition that the state has a right to conduct, as well as to support, schools. Yet this pamphlet "precipitated an educational controversy among Catholics which was without parallel in American Catholic history . . . Bouquillon's views were greeted with a storm of criticism which clearly showed that . . . they were out of harmony with the views held by most American Catholics." (Burns: "Growth and Development of the Catholic School System.") Monsignor Satolli, who came to represent the pope at the Chicago Exposition, delivered fourteen points on education without allaying the tempest, and made public a letter from the pope which gave alarm because it seemed to countenance Bouquillon's views and weaken the decrees of the Baltimore Council. We see the interesting spectacle of American Catholicism quite definitely apprehensive lest the pope should be taking too liberal a position on the school question. The pope sent another letter stating that he had no intention of abrogating any part of the Baltimore decrees as to the necessity of completely Catholic schools. Such compromises as the Faribault plan might be approved under exceptional conditions, but they did not represent the ideal.

So it seems to remain the dominant opinion that, as Brownson and Burns both clearly say, the state has really no right to educate at all, though the pope refrained from making a definite pronouncement on that theoretical point, contenting himself with the reiteration of the law that the parishes must establish schools and that Catholic children must attend them.

Besides parochial schools in about 7,000 parishes, the Catholic educational system includes 179 colleges for boys, 732 academies for girls, and 141 seminaries for training for the priesthood with nearly 14,000 students.

CATHOLIC LESSONS IN CITIZENSHIP

Protestants are legitimately interested in knowing what is taught to the more than two millions of their future fellow-citizens who are in these schools and what has been taught to the other millions who have passed through them in recent years. The decision of the United States Supreme Court in the Oregon school case invalidated the law requiring the attendance of all children at the public schools, but it explicitly affirmed: "No question is raised concerning the power of the state to regulate all schools, and to require....and that nothing be taught which is manifestly inimical to the public welfare."

Mr. Charles C. Marshall's thorough study of "The Roman Catholic Church in the Modern State" (Dodd, Mead & Co., 1928) has been published since this book was written and partly put into type. I take the liberty of taking from it the following quotation from the "Course of Religious Instruction, Institute of the Brothers of the Christian Schools, Manual of Christian Doctrine. Authorized English version. Revised in accordance with the Code of 1918. 48th edition McVey, Philadelphia, 1926." It bears the imprimatur of D. J. Dougherty, Archbishop of Philadelphia, 1918.

Q. Why are the qualities of the Church superior to those of civil society, or the State?
A. Because the Church is a religious and supernatural society, while the State is temporal and natural. The Church is a universal, immutable and immortal society, while the State is particular, variable and temporal.
Q. Why is the Church independent of the State?
A. Because its origin, authority, object and end are not from the State; because Christ himself willed that his Church, like himself, should be independent of all earthly power.
Q. Why is the Church superior to the State?
A. Because the end to which the Church tends is the noblest of all ends.
Q. In what order or respect is the State subordinate to the Church?
A. In the spiritual order and in all things referring to that order.

Q. What right has the pope in virtue of this supremacy?

A. The right to annul those laws or acts of government that would injure the salvation of souls or attack the natural rights of citizens.

Q. What more should the State do than respect the rights and liberties of the Church?

A. The State should also aid, protect and defend the Church.

Q. Has the State the right and the duty to proscribe schism and heresy?

A. Yes, it has the right and the duty to do both for the good of the nation and for that of the faithful themselves; for religious unity is the principal foundation of social unity.

Q. When may the State tolerate dissenting worship?

A. When these worships have acquired a sort of legal existence consecrated by time and accorded by treaties or covenants.

Q. May the State separate itself from the Church?

A. No, because it may not withdraw from the supreme rule of Christ.

Q. What name is given to the doctrine that the State has neither the right nor the duty to be united to the Church to protect it?

A. This doctrine is called *Liberalism*. It is founded principally on the fact that modern society rests on liberty of conscience and of worship, on liberty of speech and of the press.

Q. Why is Liberalism to be condemned?

A. 1. Because it denies all subordination of the State to the Church; 2. Because it confounds liberty with right; 3. Because it despises the social dominion of Christ, and rejects the benefits derived therefrom.

The Brothers of the Christian Schools publish this text-book "as a manual of religious instruction not only in the novitiates and scholasticates of teaching Congregations, but also in the classes of high schools, academies and colleges." The extent to which this teaching is a suitable preparation for loyal American citizenship is a matter which the reader can judge for himself.

CATHOLICS IN PUBLIC LIFE

In spite of the closely knit organization of the Catholic church, its centralized control, its avowed interest in some matters which are determined by political methods, and the recurrent suspicion that it exerts undue influence in getting what it wants, it has either not been unduly solicitous to get its own members into public office or has not been conspicuously successful in doing so. The number of members of the leading denominations in the House of Representatives and the Senate respectively (according to the Methodist Board of Temperance, Prohibition and Public Morals, Jan. 16, 1928) is as follows: Methodists, 94, 32; Presbyterians, 64, 8; Episcopalians, 51, 24; Baptists, 51, 6; Congregationalists, 26, 7; Disciples, 20, 1; Lutherans, 16, 2; Roman Catholic, 35, 6. In the House there are 347 with Protestant affiliations, and 35 Catholics; in the Senate, 86 Protestants and 5 Catholics. A Catholic correspondent of "America" complains: "We, as Catholics, are a negligible quantity in the life of the nation today, if the number of important offices of public trust which Catholics hold is any criterion of the influence which they exert."

The record in municipal politics would probably have quite a different color. Both their numerical representation and their influence there has been much greater.

There are something over 70 weekly Catholic papers published in the United States, including such ably edited journals as "America," which is under Jesuit auspices, and "The Commonweal," which is in the hands of laymen. A news service conducted by the National Catholic Welfare Council furnishes news to Catholic papers.

NEW CATHOLIC ACTIVITIES

Catholic propaganda activities in both Europe and America have taken on new vigor since the war. The reasons for this need not detain us. The fact is obvious. On the side of organization, the data are most fully presented in *"L'Union Catholique,"* by Albert Bessières (Paris, 1924), with an introduction by the Bishop of Versailles. "In the international field," says this author, "the church has encouraged the formation of international federations of students, of Catholic youth, of Catholic leagues of women, of Christian workmen, the international union of social studies, the apostolic league of nations, and the International Catholic league, which had a congress at Constance in August, 1923. In the national field, the Holy See has encouraged national federations of Catholic youth, of Catholic men, of Catholic women, and such organizations as the German Volksverein, the Italian Catholic popular union, and the National Catholic Welfare Council in the United States."

In France, the annual Catholic congresses, which began thirty years ago, and the Catholic committee of religious defense, have led to something much more intricate and effective. The Bishop of Versailles outlines a plan, which has partly been carried into effect, for a system of diocesan, cantonal and parish unions containing bureaux, secretariats and committees having to do with matters of religion, education, press and propaganda, youth, and charitable and social matters, and constituting "a powerful and benevolent national Catholic federation." The achievements of similar organizations in Germany and Holland are cited. The efficiency of the National Catholic Welfare Council in the United States is held up as an example to be emulated by other countries.

Of great importance in Europe is the elaborate system of organizations known collectively as Catholic Action. This first took definite form in Italy in 1923 after the dissolution of the Popular party, which had been largely Catholic. Under the patronage of the pope, new organizations of laymen were formed and these and the older ones were consolidated under clerical guidance, with the general title *Azione Cattolica Italiana*. Parochial committees and diocesan committees head up in a central council under a president selected by the pope. The policy of Catholic Action is to avoid entanglement with political parties— as is obviously wise under present conditions in Italy —but to weld its members into "a mobilized army" for the achievement of such social, moral and religious ends as are approved by the church. Among its objectives are welfare work among the needy classes, the maintenance of Catholic standards of morality, the religious education of the young, and, in general, "the re-Christianization of our life" through the activity of a "lay apostolate" working under clerical direction. One of its leaders says: "The Catholic Action is the only salvation from the chaos with which the world is today afflicted." Similar movements have been started in Austria, Czechoslovakia and Poland, and in the new concordat between Lithuania and the Papal See the state specifically agrees to give full liberty to "organizations which, following mainly religious purposes, comprise part of the Catholic Action and as such are dependent upon the authority of the bishop." (Prof. Heinrich Hermelink, of Marburg, in *Die christliche Welt*, Feb. 18, 1928.)

The National Catholic Welfare Council was organized in 1919. It grew out of a congress of twenty-seven Catholic organizations, held in Washington in 1917, which led first to the National Catholic War Council. In 1921 the Archbishop of San Francisco, reporting for the Council, said: "In eight months we have coordinated and united the Catholic power of this country. It now knows where and when to act, and is encouraged by the consciousness of its unity. We feel ourselves powerful because our union has become visible. All our Catholic organizations report an increase of energy and do not doubt that, thanks to the N. C. W. C., we can bring Catholic cooperation to its apogee."

It has departments, each presided over by a bishop, on education, legislation, social action, lay organizations, and the press, and an executive department which "keeps itself in direct contact with the government, to which it makes known the Catholic point of view on legislation such as the prohibition bill, the tariff and the classification of religious objects." (Bressières, page 193.) "The department of education has been consulted by the War department in the selection of professors for the schools in the Philippines. The judicial department is frequently consulted by the government and by the authorities of the several states." (Bressières, p. 194.)

The National Council of Catholic Men "has several million members. It has already led several campaigns, notably against the encroachment of the state in the field of education. During 1923 it is to concentrate its activity upon two points: the cinema and immigration." (Bressières, p. 195.)

The Knights of Columbus, organized in 1882, have taken on new vigor since the war, not only in their original activity of supporting Catholic education and in providing for Catholic young men those facilities which the Y. M. C. A. has made familiar and popular, but in directly combating the influence of the Y in certain European countries, notably in Italy, and in creating sentiment with reference to the alleged persecution of the Catholic church in Mexico.

PROPAGANDA AND CONVERSIONS

The output of Catholic propaganda literature both in English and in the European languages, during the past few years has been greatly enlarged. Much of it is of excellent literary quality, prepared especially with a view to presenting the Catholic system as in harmony with all that is best in modern thought and

opposed only to "science falsely so called" and to what
is dangerous and destructive in current social and
intellectual tendencies. Much attention is also given
to the lives and experiences of converts and to the
portrayal of the processes by which they have been led
to Rome.

A notable and highly intelligent effort to influence
the thinking of both Catholics and non-Catholics by
guiding their reading is the *"Office Centrale de Li-
brairie et Bibliographie"* at Paris. This is an organization which not only sells books but publishes a comprehensive magazine of book-reviews and occasional
classified lists and furnishes bibliographical service on
every conceivable topic. Its procedure is precisely the
opposite of the Index of prohibited books. The more
intelligent a person is, the more he is likely to resent
being told what he must not read, but the more he
will appreciate competent advice as to what he can
advantageously read. The *Office Centrale* does not
flaunt the word "Catholic" in its name or on its literature, but it takes good care to recommend only those
books which contain nothing contrary to the Catholic
point of view. This is an effective and thoroughly
legitimate piece of propaganda. The organization of
a "Catholic literary guild" in the United States has
been announced (April, 1928) to supplement the work
of the parochial schools by encouraging the circulation
of Catholic books and giving systematic warnings
against "pagan" books.

The Catholic Directory for 1927 estimates that

about 30,000 non-Catholics became converts to Catholicism in the United States in the preceding year. Shaughnessy's estimate of the total number of converts since 1790 is 830,000. If these figures are even approximately correct, it does not appear that Catholicism is making great gains outside of its own ranks. The ratio of converts for the year to the total number of Catholics is about one to 650. But even that number is enough to make it pertinent to ask, what is that "lure of Rome" to which we often hear reference and which is felt by vastly more than the number of those who yield to it? What kinds of people are they who "make their submission" to Rome? The following analysis is intended to be suggestive rather than complete. It will reveal the point of view of one who is not insensitive to some aspects of that "lure" but who is convinced that Rome does not give all that the lure seems to promise.

THE "LURE" OF ROME

The logical appeal of Rome is to absolutists, who think of truth as an unalterable finality, a deposit delivered once for all, needing only to be incorruptibly preserved and infallibly declared. If it be conceded that it was the will of God and of Christ to give men a complete body of permanent truth with reference to the doctrines of religion and the obligations of morality, then it may be plausibly argued—as Catholic apologists do argue—that God *must* have established a church and endowed it with supernatural power to receive, preserve and declare that truth. What other organization is there, except the Catholic church, which even claims to be so endowed? With one tremendous, world-wide, and age-long church asserting that it has such an endowment and presenting a single system of dogma as the content of that God-given truth, and a multitude of much smaller ones offering diverse systems based upon their varying interpretations of the Bible, all comparatively recent, and still others holding that truth must be endlessly sought and only partially, though increasingly, apprehended, it is not to be wondered at that the seeker of an absolute and comprehensive revelation should turn hopefully to the church which makes the greatest claim. The church existed before the New Testament. Jesus neither wrote, nor gave instructions to his immediate disciples to write a systematic and final statement of his doctrines. The New Testament, even if inerrant, and even if it contains the materials for such a system, evidently does not contain the system itself stated with unmistakable meaning. To many, it seems evident from the New Testament that Jesus had no interest in leaving behind him any such system, whether in written form or to be gradually unfolded and declared by an infallible church. But for those who believe that such a system of absolute truth is essential to the salvation of souls, and that therefore he *must* have taken every precaution to make it as inerrant and as authoritative as possible, the argument for the Roman Catholic position must have very great weight. To summarize the argument of Belloc: You either have a church or you do not. If you do, you have an authority which can, at any time, declare what is the absolute truth. If you do not, you have no positive and unchangeable norm of truth and are a prey to varying moods and opinions.

Tired minds and timid minds, which shrink from the responsibility of deciding upon difficult questions of belief, gladly pass over that responsibility to an organization which makes such positive, not to say arrogant, assertion of its own competence. Men seek to avoid responsibility almost as anxiously as to escape danger. A life-long Baptist who had become a convert to Rome testified to a peace of mind never experienced before. "I was always troubled by doubts before; I didn't know whether I was saved or not; now I can turn those doubts all over to the church." "But suppose the church should be wrong?" "Well, anyway, it won't be my fault." These are they who find—as many a civilian did when he joined the army—that there is a certain comfort in having someone else make the decisions. Submission to authority has its compensations.

Akin to these are the distracted, the despairing and the bereaved, whose intellectual processes have broken down in the presence of some overwhelming disappointment or calamity. Finding not only their own resources inadequate but their independent capacity for assimilating help from invisible sources too weak, they turn, like hurt children, to "mother church" as affording tangible means of laying hold upon comfort and power. When critical processes are in abeyance and the hand is groping blindly for something to grasp, a patron saint represented as visibly present and promising aid, a kindly Madonna nearer and more human than an invisible Christ, yet all-powerful in intercession at the heavenly throne, an altar at which to kneel with that "stoop of the soul which in bending upraises it too," a confessional, perhaps, in which to unburden the conscience of its guilty load—these seem acceptable instruments of release to the oppressed spirit. One may think that there are better ways, but not to realize that these are tempting paths to peace for such a one is not to know how troubled minds work.

Conservatives in an age of social and institutional instability inevitably seek the reinforcement of the most conservative institution they know, as storm-tossed sailors seek the shelter of a harbor. It has been so in every turbulent age. It was the growing institutional solidarity of the papacy which gave it such value as it had in the age when the Roman Empire was dissolving into chaos. When the rising spirit of nationalism and the turmoil of the renaissance and the reformation threatened the dissolution of the old order, the forces of reaction rallied around the church as the symbol of conservatism. When the French revolution and the innovations of the upstart Corsican put the vested interests of property and rank into such peril as they had not suffered since the barbarian

invasions, the first thought of the conservative states-
men who undertook to restore so much of the old
regime as had not been irrevocably swept away was
to rebuild the power of the church and of the "legitimate" dynasties. Throughout the first half of the
nineteenth century, all those who opposed democracy
as the synonym for anarchy pointed to the church as
the bulwark against revolution. And since the Great
War, Catholicism has made the same appeal to those
who fear the new liberalism in religion, in social ideals,
in moral standards, in political organization. Bolshevism is the favorite bogey-man now. To quote
a correspondent in "The Commonweal" (Aug. 10,
1927): "Catholicism is the one and only bulwark
against bolshevism and kindred isms." How much
actual danger there is from "bolshevism and kindred
isms" need not here be discussed. But the fact is that,
when any radicalism on a large scale is in the air,
the natural—though not necessarily the wisest—reaction of conservatives is toward the most stable and
conservative institution in sight. Whatever may be
the merits or defects of Catholicism, it is just that—
the most stable and the most conservative institution
in the world at the present time, as well as the oldest,
the largest, and the most autocratic.

THE APPEAL OF PARADOX

Catholicism makes a curiously paradoxical appeal
to some very modern and practical men who, while
they have no patience with discussions of dogma, and

even because of that fact, find themselves admiring the Catholic church because it imposes its dogmas without argument and goes about its practical business with a high degree of efficiency. For example, Bruce Barton—surely modern enough—in "What Can a Man Believe" says: "The Catholic Church on the whole is doing its task successfully . . . No man of reverent spirit can pass its altars without bowing his head . . . The Protestant church presents a confused and baffling picture." And again: "The church is too often rigid and unadaptable. I speak now particularly of the Protestant church; the Roman Catholic church has shown a deeper knowledge of human nature and more capacity for giving the people what the people really need . . . I am a Protestant of a score of generations. It is impossible for me intellectually to be a Catholic; spiritually I wish often that I might be." Minds of this type do not often, I think, go the full length of submission to Rome, but their frank admiration of the business efficiency of the church and its complete commitment to its own program, and of the adaptations to the impulses of human nature which it finds consistent with absolute refusal to adapt its doctrines or organization to modern thought, increases the prestige of the church and makes the submission of others easier.

There is an appeal—equally paradoxical—to temperamental insurgents and heretics who rebel against whatever orthodoxies are most insistently thrust upon them and who, in this case, find the orthodoxies of the intelligentsia in an age of science more irksome than the dogmas of faith. Rationalism, secularism, art-for-art's-sake were the conventional respectabilities in English intellectual circles a few years ago. G. K. Chesterton rebelled and championed philistinism and Catholic dogma. The ultimate act of rebellion is to rebel against rebellion itself and to return to authority when lesser rebels are satisfied with liberty. "The act of defending any of the cardinal virtues has today all the exhilaration of a vice," says Chesterton. In similar vein Bernard Shaw—though a socialist, not a Catholic—recounts a parallel experience: "I was ready to grasp at everything new. At that time I refused to believe a word of the Bible and was ready to accept every new theory any scientist offered. Today I would rather believe the story of Jonah and the whale than a fact almost proved by a scientist." (N. Y. Times, Aug. 7, 1927.) Minds especially susceptible to argument from paradox are singularly impressed by the claim of the Catholic church to be the true home of freedom.

HUNGRY FOR COLOR

More potent than any single item in the above list, perhaps, is the appeal to color-starved moderns whose own lives are commonplace but who yearn for pomp and pageantry. The mood of the romantic mediaevalist slumbers in the background of even prosaic and realistic souls, and sometimes it awakens to clamor for satisfaction. John Citizen has schooled himself to wear a gray suit of ready-made clothes and a derby and to carry an umbrella, but there are certain cells of his brain that yearn for a plumed hat, a jeweled sword-hilt, and golden spurs. He lives behind roller-shades of unobtrusive tint, but part of him longs for floating banners, yellow, glorious, golden, with splashes of crimson and dashes of blue. He loves his flat or his bungalow, but all of him cannot live there. He does not know it—though the people who build the newer motion-picture theatres know it—but he is starved for color, and something in him responds gratefully when it is offered to him either by a circus parade or by a cardinal's procession.

The collocation of these items is not intended to belittle ecclesiastical ostentation. It is a legitimate hunger, and the satisfaction of it is a legitimate satisfaction.

But from the standpoint of the Catholic Church itself, the motive behind its displays of magnificence is something quite different from that. It connects directly with the concept of the church as the supreme authority. The purpose is to give to the functionaries of the church a visible setting which, without argument or controversy, will proclaim to the eye the importance, the uniqueness, the authority of the church. People will believe almost anything if it can be told to them without putting them into a controversial mood. So, embroidered vestments, solemn music and clouds of incense, appealing to eye and ear and nostril rather than to reason, make the church appear commanding and authoritative.

We do the same thing in a more somber mode when we dress the supreme court in robes, and in brighter tones when we give military officers uniforms and insignia and hold parades with bands and flags. These things are not stimulants to patriotism but incentives to obedience. Ecclesiastical magnificence is not an aid to devotion but an inducement to submission.

A cardinal entered Chicago on his return from Rome—the first cardinal Chicago ever had. Miles of parade, miles of bunting, thousands of flags, streets roped-off, surface cars re-routed, platoons of police, a triumphal procession for the "prince of the church" through throngs to whom he imparted his blessing with uplifted fingers. Then a great ceremony in the cathedral, a ceremony made brilliant and colorful by every ecclesiastical device and every available item of regalia. A long description of the vestments used in the pontifical high mass recites the splendor of the copes and mitres, and closes by mentioning the coat-of-arms of the cardinal, with the insignia of the Virgin, a shining star, golden bees, a crown, and one word— *Humilitas!*

The right word to bring such a description to a focus is not *humilitas*, but *auctoritas*. But the color-starved romantic mediaevalist is not thinking primarily of that. What he wants is color. But what he gets is authority.

X

WORSHIP, SHRINES AND MIRACLES

Catholicism as a system of worship has developed a highly elaborated technique of devotion. Its characteristic features are the use of holy objects as the physical vehicles through which spiritual blessings are dispensed, the performance of specified routines for the expression or evocation of religious sentiments, and the invocation of holy persons as mediators between God and man. The first of these categories includes relics of the saints, images, holy water, scapulars and medals; the second, the use of the rosary with its many repetitions of the *Ave Maria* and the *Pater Noster*, the observance of the canonical hours of devotion, the religious pilgrimages, the stations of the cross; the third, the veneration of the saints and of the Virgin Mary as intercessors.

In theory, and very often in practice, it is highly mystical, the symbols and objects furnishing the means of approach to a vivid sense of direct communion with God. If sometimes the mind of the worshipper lingers upon the symbol or rambles off to irrelevant matters while the body is performing a familiar routine, this is not unlike what happens also in those forms of religion which employ a simpler technique and less elaborate paraphernalia of worship. Even

Protestant minds may wander during the singing of a hymn or during the "long prayer."

The central act of worship is the mass. In it, history, dogma and devotion meet. History, because it is understood to be a continuation of the great historical fact of Christianity, the sacrifice of Christ, and because its use and development run through the whole history of the church from very early times. Dogma, because it is an embodiment of the doctrine of transubstantiation. Devotion, because it is the most important and effective item in the program of worship; so much so that one might say that, while every other form of worship is optional for a Catholic, the mass is obligatory.

THE MIRACLE OF THE MASS

The mass is sometimes described as a dramatization of the events upon Calvary. This is not quite accurate; it does not do full justice to the seriousness with which it is taken. The essential act is not drama but reality. The mass is a continuation of the sacrifice of Christ. How is this possible? Because sacrifice includes two elements: the death of the victim, which in this case was accomplished once for all on Calvary; and the offering of the victim, which can be repeated indefinitely as the bread and wine become the actual body and blood of Christ and are offered upon the altar.

The doctrine of transubstantiation, or the teaching that the bread and wine become, in the act of consecration, the actual and real body and blood of Christ, is therefore the central doctrine of Catholicism considered as a system of worship, as the affirmation of the supreme authority and infallibility of the pope is its central doctrine when considered as a system of religious government. The power of performing that miracle of transubstantiation is the thing that distinguishes the priest from the layman. This is the reason why the Catholic church cannot recognize the validity of the priestly orders of any other church, such as the Anglican, aside from their failing to give obedience to Rome. A priest whose ordination does not empower him to work this miracle of the changed substance—and how can it if neither the church nor the priest believe in that miracle?—cannot be a "mass-priest," and no other sort is a real priest in the view of Catholics.

But how *can* Catholics believe a thing so contrary to reason and the plain evidence of the senses as that bread becomes flesh? Before calling it so utterly irrational and summoning the testimony of the senses to refute it, consider two things. In the first place a miracle is a miracle. If one is sufficiently embued with the idea that the whole fabric of religion is woven of miracles, and that physical miracles are a matter of constant occurrence, it is no great strain upon credulity to believe that God not only performs this miracle but performs it in such a way that the evidences of it are hidden from sight. It is just as easy for divine omnipotence to change bread to body that looks like bread as it would be to change it to body that looks like body. This is doubtless all the uneducated Catholic feels that he needs to know about it. To him it seems more reasonable that a thing of this sort should occur, inexplicable as it is, along with all the other miracles which he believes are constantly going on, than that the omnipotent and infallible church which teaches it should be wrong. It is true because the church teaches that it is true.

But if a philosopher asks, how?—there is an answer for him also. Objects consist of *qualities,* such as color, extension, hardness, and so on, which are apprehended by the senses, and *substance,* which is that unseen something which, as the word implies, stands under the qualities and holds them together. Observation, even if it extends to chemical analysis, can never reach anything but qualities. Substance lies in a deeper stratum of reality. I will not pause to criticize this metaphysic. It does not seem to me to be tenable, but it involves no logical impossibility. It is one which mediaeval philosophers held and which appeals to many now as being a common-sense conception of the nature of things. Keep it in mind: qualities inhering in substance—like pins stuck in a pin-cushion so thickly that only the pins are visible and the cushion is perfectly and permanently concealed.

Now it is the substance that is changed, not the qualities. The qualities remain the qualities of bread and wine, and no amount of minute observation can conceivably detect any alteration, for, by definition, whatever is observed is merely a quality. But the substance, the unknown and empirically unknowable essence, is changed into the substance of the body and blood of Christ. It requires a miracle to do this, of course, but it is a miracle which takes place beyond the reach of the senses. Granted the conception of a God who is continually performing miracles for the benefit of the faithful, it does not seem inconceivable that he should perform this one if substance and qualities are in theory separable.

But why should one believe that he does perform it? First, because the church teaches that he does. Second, because the words of Jesus as given in the gospels, if literally interpreted, say that he does, and the church, which is the authorized interpreter of Scripture, says that this is what his words mean.

THE BEAUTIES OF THE MASS

While the mass is not essentially a drama but a real sacrifice, many of the details which have been built up around its central act are dramatic representations of the events by which the original sacrifice was surrounded. It is therefore an intensely impressive service of worship when understood, symbolical or dramatic in its preparatory details but rising to the most poignant reality at its focal point. As a body of devotional literature nearly all of its text is excellent. At least three-fourths of it is biblical. Its general structure—with its successive preparation

of the heart and mind, its offerings, consecration and
communion—is the wise product of centuries of study
of the art of worship. There are a few references to
Mary and the saints which Protestants will find foreign to their interests, and many minute directions
as to posture, vestments and incense, all significant
as symbols but striking the Protestant mind as being
too detailed and petty, as though God cared for attitudes, embroidery and perfume.

It is in Latin, easy to read but mostly unintelligible
as usually rendered. Probably those beautiful features
of the mass which a Protestant will approve as he
reads it do not enter at all into the consciousness of
ninety-nine per cent of the devout Catholic communicants. The Latin words are not intended to convey
specific ideas; they are a sort of vocal incense, or
verbal music. What does enter into consciousness to
the exclusion of every other feature is the belief that
a miracle is being enacted before their eyes, that by
virtue of that miracle God is really, corporeally, and
in a sense visibly present upon the altar. Here is a
new incarnation, and a continuance of the sacrifice
by virtue of which their salvation is purchased. It
is not strange that such a service should be deemed
profoundly important by those who believe the doctrines which underlie it, and that a church which is
the custodian of such holy mysteries and a priesthood
at whose hands such a saving and sacramental miracle
can be performed should be reverenced as the embodiment of divine authority.

Thus the authority of the church as a disciplinary and governing body and the sense of the vividness and reality of the presence of God in the mass mutually reinforce each other. The faithful believe in the mass because the church teaches it, and they submit the more willingly to the church because it holds the treasure of the mass.

The doctrine of the real presence of Christ in the consecrated elements makes possible not only the sacrifice in the mass but also the adoration of Christ in the wafer at other times, as when it is preserved upon the altar or carried in procession. To understand the genuineness of this adoration it must be realized that the wafer does not become the dead body of Christ but his living body in which his living spirit and personality are resident as truly as they were in that body which walked by the lake in Galilee and trod the Via Dolorosa.

The eucharistic congresses, the first of which was held at Lille, France, in 1881 and the twenty-eighth in Chicago in 1926, are gatherings designed to manifest and stimulate devotion to Christ as embodied in the sacrament, and incidentally to promote morale within the church and increase its prestige outside. The eucharistic congress in Chicago was probably the largest assembly ever held for purely devotional purposes.

OBJECTS OF RELIGION

The employment of religious objects, such as relics, images, medals, holy water and rosaries, has an important place in the program of Catholic piety, but the efficacy of these things rests upon an entirely different basis from that of the consecrated wafer. The relics of the saints are believed to retain something of the sanctity of the saints themselves and to be the means by which their "heroic virtues" may become efficacious for the spiritual or physical welfare of those who venerate them. Images of the saints are considered sacred only in the sense that they have been set apart for a sacred purpose. In general, they are venerated only in a sense somewhat analogous to that in which one venerates the flag, or the picture of one's mother, and their utility is that they fix the attention and stimulate the imagination of the worshipper. These analogies, however, are quite inadequate to describe the degree of reverence paid to certain pictures and images—such as that of Our Lady of Guadalupe, Mexico, or the Black Virgin of Einsiedeln, Switzerland—to which a miraculous origin and miraculous powers are ascribed.

The rosary, while it may acquire a special virtue by being blessed, has a psychological value in that its 165 beads, divided into fifteen decades representing the fifteen mysteries of the faith, are designed to furnish a guide, a stimulus, and a restraint to the thoughts of the worshipper in his private devotions. A guide, because through training and association each bead has its definite meaning and therefore gives the mind as well as the fingers something to hold to. A stimulus, because there are just so many beads to be told and one cannot stop before the end without being definitely aware that he has cut short the allotted period of his devotions. A restraint, because the presence of the physical symbol in the hands helps to recall the vagrant thoughts of the worshipper from those meanderings into which thoughts so easily diverge when we essay to fix them upon supersensuous objects.

Perhaps the most important of the religious duties of the Catholic is confession. Although not a sacrament, it is closely connected with penance, which is listed among the seven sacraments. (The seven are: baptism, confirmation, eucharist, penance, matrimony, extreme unction, holy orders.) No other obligation is more constantly stressed than that of confession. Its importance springs from the fact that sins are forgiven only on condition of being confessed to a priest. To die with mortal sins unconfessed is to die with these sins unforgiven, and that means damnation. Frequent confession is recommended. At least annual confession is commanded. To carry unconfessed sins over Easter is a grave breach of discipline.

Since psycho-analysis came into vogue, much has been said of the psychological value of confession in curing sick souls by the release of repressions and by opening and draining the sores that sin has made and secrecy has sealed. There is something in it. It has been plausibly argued that Protestantism also needs a counterpart of the confessional. On the other hand, as pointed out by Dr. E. Boyd Barrett who, as a Jesuit priest, has had much experience on both sides of the grating, confession is better adapted to secure the control of the church over the penitent than to win peace for him; it creates as many neuroses as it cures; instead of removing doubts and fears, it often leads to an exaggerated fear lest one has made a "bad" confession and so incurred additional guilt. (Article, "The Drama of Catholic Confession," The Journal of Religion, April, 1928.) Whatever may be the actual balance of debits and credits for confession with reference to the health of souls, it is unquestionably a potent instrument for securing submission. Like all potent instruments, it is liable to abuse.

MODERN MIRACLES

The cult of the saints and of the Virgin Mary has acquired rather than lost popularity since the beginning of the nineteenth century. Saints are still being canonized in large numbers. According to the *"Annuaire Pontifical Catholique"* for 1926, six new saints were added to the roll during the preceding year, and 125 persons were "beatified." The greater number of the beatified consisted of three groups of martyrs— 8 Jesuits of Canada, 32 martyrs at Orange during the French revolution, and 79 Korean martyrs of 1839-1846. In the case of those separately canonized and beatified, proof of two miracles for each was received and approved by the Congregation of Rites.

During the last hundred years there has been a new regime of miracles, apparitions, stigmatizations and the like. The case of Louise Lateau, in Belgium in 1868, involved both trance and stigmatization (the appearance of the five wounds of Christ on hands, feet and side). She could be awakened from her trance only by her bishop or someone authorized by him. The condition continued for some years. Later, when her bishop deserted the ultramontane party in the Kulturkampf, she was threatened with excommunication. During the last years of her life she was a brain-shattered invalid.

In Alsace-Lorraine there was an epidemic of apparitions of the Virgin beginning in 1872 and lasting about two years. Crowds of people at scores of places claimed to see such apparitions.

The case of the miraculous cure of Pierre de Rudder, in 1875, is discussed at length by G. H. Joyce, S. J., in "The Question of Miracles" (p. 122, sqq).

A case of stigmatization in Germany is being currently reported in Catholic periodicals and is now (1928) being officially investigated.

The Catholic view of the activities of spirits is suggested not only by the bulls of seventeenth century popes against witchcraft, and by the statement (Montague Summers: "The Geography of Witchcraft," p. 571) that "during the whole of the eighteenth century the belief in witchcraft was universal throughout Italy," but by this more nearly contemporary opinion: "Catholic demonology, so long derided by the scientific world, has been verified by the phenomena of spiritualism, now accredited by such a leading scientist as Sir Oliver Lodge." (E. I. Watkin, of New College, Oxford: "Some Thoughts on Catholic Apologetics." London, 1915, with the *nihil obstat* and *imprimatur*.)

The use of amulets and scapulars as a defense against such dangers as falls, fires, drowning and sickness, is still encouraged. (I can remember wondering about the little cloth tags which certain boyish comrades used to wear around their necks when we went swimming.) Of a Benedictine medal it was officially declared in 1876 that it "cures sickness, relieves toothache, stops nose-bleed, heals burns, overcomes craving for drink, protects from evil spirits, restrains skittish horses, cures sick cattle, clears vineyards of blight, and secures the conversion of heretics and godless persons." (Tract entitled *"St. Benediktusbuchlein oder die Medaille d. h. Benediktus."* Munster, 1876. Quoted in Kurtz: Church History, III, 248.)

Lest the Protestant become too superior, he may be reminded that Gov. Winthrop wrote, in 1656: "For all sorts of agewes, I have of late tryed the following magneticall experiment with infallible success. Pare the patients nayles when the fever is coming on; and put the paringes into a little bagge of fine linen or sarenet; and tye that about a live eeles necke, in a tubbe of water. The eel will dye and the patient will recover." But that was two hundred years earlier. And anyway, the two are not parallel. Winthrop's "Magneticall experiment" was a medical folly. The medal is supposed to operate by purely miraculous means.

RELICS AND SHRINES

New relics of ancient saints have been discovered in recent times and their identification has been assisted by their miracle-working powers. The catacombs of Rome have been the chief, though not the only, source of the supply. Bones of St. Francis, Santa Clara, St. Ambrose, the martyrs Gervasius and Protasius, and the Apostles Philip and James the Less, all lately discovered, were vouched for by Pius VII and Pius IX. In 1870 the skeleton of the Apostle James the Elder was found in the crypt of the church which he was supposed to have founded, St. Iago de Campostella. The investigation extended over years, and the identification was approved by Leo XIII, November, 1884, in an apostolic brief in which he extolled the merits of the bones of the saints. (The story of the relics of St. James is much more complicated than this too brief summary would indicate. It is told in all its ramifications and contradictions by Rev. James S. Stone in "The Cult of Santiago," London, 1927.)

The increasing importance of the Virgin Mary in Catholic devotions reached its climax in the promulgation of the dogma of the Immaculate Conception in 1854 by Pius IX. The meaning of this dogma is that the Virgin Mary was, from the first moment of her conception, miraculously preserved from the least stain of original sin. It has nothing whatever to do with the doctrine of the virgin birth of Jesus, to which the term is sometimes ignorantly applied. The companion-piece to this doctrine is the Assumption of the Virgin—that is, that her body was carried to heaven after her death. This is a pious belief but has never been officially proclaimed as a dogma of the faith; the difference being that one can deny it without incurring damnation, though not without "insolent temerity," since it is generally accepted by the church. As there is no evidence on the subject that even the pious imagination could call historical, the belief comes as near as possible to being an act of pure faith.

The supreme manifestation of Catholic belief in physical miracles at the present day is found in connection with such world-famous shrines as Ste. Anne de Beauprè in Quebec, Guadalupe in Mexico, Einsiedeln in Switzerland, and—greatest of all—Lourdes in southern France. At each of these the thousands of votive offerings, the mountains of abandoned crutches, and the tablets recording singular mercies—ranging from the winning of a law-suit to falling uninjured from a fourth-story window 'and the instantaneous cure of broken bones and open sores—attest the belief of the faithful in the efficacy of intercession to the saint or the particular manifestation of the Virgin which is honored at these shrines.

The strictly contemporary character of this belief in special providences dispensed through the saints, as well as the variety of needs that are satisfied, is evidenced by an account of the rapidly increasing popularity of the shrine of St. Anthony at Graymoor, N. Y., in the "Catholic Citizen" (April, 1927). Testimonials are published from satisfied clients who report health restored, employment found, "the success of a new business location," and other favors. "My son has come home and I feel sure that it was only through the intercession of St. Anthony and your help that the miracle happened." "My little boy's bicycle was taken off our porch. I thought of St. Anthony and started a novena to him, promising an offering of thanksgiving if the bicycle would be found. The very next day, while walking on the avenue, we saw some children playing with it, and we feel sure that it was St. Anthony who guided our steps in that direction." Thus a system of belief which, at first sight, might seem other-worldly and remote, is brought into intimate relation to the most concrete and even commonplace interests.

OUR LADY OF LOURDES

Singularly enough, as it may seem, the most popular of all the great shrines and the one to which the highest sanctity and efficacy are attributed, is the one of most recent origin. For it was only in 1858 that the Virgin Mary appeared to Bernadette Soubirous (beatified in 1925), a peasant girl of Lourdes, and said "I am the Immaculate Conception." This was a timely apparition, for it was only four years after the promulgation of the dogma. Bernadette saw the vision eighteen times, but no one else ever saw it at all, or heard, as she did, the command to tell the priests to build a chapel there and visit the grotto with processions. Neighbors flocked to see the place of the vision. A miraculous spring burst forth. A blind peasant whose eyes had been destroyed by an explosion in a mine had his sight restored by application of the water. In vain the local authorities, not knowing what greatness was in store for the community, tried to discourage the pilgrimages. The church itself was in no hurry to accept and guarantee the miracle and the cures. Too many alleged apparitions in the years immediately preceding had been proved fraudulent. After four years, when about thirty cures had been reported, the Bishop of Tarbes attested the authenticity of the appearance of the Virgin and approved the pilgrimages. Papal approval was secured in 1872. Bernadette took the veil, died at the age of thirty-four, and Lourdes became the greatest healing shrine and place of pilgrimage in the Catholic world.

I visited Lourdes in 1926, coming down to it from the High Pyrenees. The snowy range is still in sight. Rounded little green mountains are all about. The Gave de Pau runs white with rapids, and beside a sharp crook in the stream is a castle-crowned crag which Charlemagne once stormed when it was held by the Moors. The old town grew up under the shelter of the castle and at the foot of the crag. But even Charlemagne is a minor character in the drama of Lourdes. In a region where half the towns were founded by the Romans and the other half have towers or churches dating at least as far back as the thirteenth century, here is a record of miracles beginning less than seventy years ago and coming down to right now. It is hard to appreciate the newness of it until one sees a shop—one of hundreds—for the sale of rosaries, crucifixes, and souvenirs, with the sign, "Pierre Soubirous, son of J. M. Soubirous, brother of Bernadette."

The grotto is the heart of Lourdes. Through it files an endless procession of pilgrims in reverent silence. Before it kneel scores, sometimes hundreds, with arms out-stretched. The sick and crippled are there by dozens, in wheel-chairs and on stretchers. There is no audible prayer, but lips move silently and there is an atmosphere of intense and concentrated supplication. The stretcher-bearers and attendants of the sick are counted by hundreds. They are volunteers serving without pay and living at their own expense. Nearly all of them are men and women apparently much above the average in culture and intelligence. Some are boy scouts.

The high points in the day are the procession and blessing of the sick in the afternoon and the procession with flambeaux in the evening. The afternoon procession, composed of two or three thousand members of organized pilgrimages from various countries, followed by long files of clergy and last of all the Holy Sacrament borne under a canopy, begins and ends in the square before the church. A hollow square is formed, lined by the sick on stretchers. The Host is carried slowly before them and each is blessed separately. Then follows a special litany for the sick, successive portions of it being in French, English, Dutch, Spanish—and whatever other languages are represented among the larger pilgrimages—and Latin. There can be few more impressive religious services in the world, and none marked by more impassioned sincerity. Five thousand people, their minds all keyed to expectation of a miracle, echo antiphonally the words of the priest: "Lord, that I may see. *Lord, that I may see.* Lord, that I may hear. *Lord, that I may hear.* Lord, that I may walk. *Lord, that I may walk.* Lord, speak but a word and my brother shall be healed." For people do not pray for themselves alone at Lourdes, but even more for each other.

A MILLION PILGRIMS A YEAR

There were no cures that day, and after the service the sick rolled away still hopeful of a delayed answer to their prayers. In fact, there are not many cures. A million pilgrims a year, probably more than a hundred thousand of them with some specific petition, and an average of less than one hundred attested cures a year. But the authorities are apparently very cautious about giving a certificate of cure. They maintain a *"Bureau des contestations medicales"* for the examination both of the sick and of the supposedly cured, and only cases which are considered indisputable are certified. No one thinks of holding the failures against Our Lady of Lourdes. She simply picks out some to be healed and passes over the others. And since the percentage of cures is known to be small, and the chance of any individual patient therefore slight, there seems to be little unfavorable reaction from disappointment.

The night procession with flambeaux is even more impressive as a spectacle than the afternoon procession. At late dusk the pilgrims gather near the grotto. A column is formed, four or six abreast, which moves up one ramp, over the lower church, down the other ramp, around the esplanade, and, when its head again reaches the square, serpentines back and forth until its whole length has been gathered into one compact mass of twinkling candles. The numbers are immense —and this was only an ordinary day. It is easy to talk loosely of "thousands," but, to be exact, it took the procession twenty-seven minutes to pass my station, and I counted two hundred passing in one measured minute. The marching pilgrims sing—badly, of course, for no procession a mile long can keep either time or pitch. But as the long wavering line coils itself into a solid mass before the church, filling the plaza, and priestly song-leaders beating time with torches give the pitch and rhythm, the diversity of tune and key is gradually converted into a splendid unison. Then follows a magnificent chanting of the credo to a Gregorian air, and the ceremony is over.

The effect of these processions is immensely impressive. Even more so is the spirit of devotion and good-will among the people. Strangely—and it *is* strange to one who knows Rome—the priests seem as humble as the people. There has been no accumulation of ecclesiastical wealth at Lourdes. There is dignity but no magnificence. There is no profiteering. There are no catch-penny devices. Even alms-boxes are few and not unduly prominent. One feels inclined to seek them out. It is probably the best place in Europe to see the lower middle class from all countries, and to see them at their best. Better than Rome it gives a sense of the international character of the Catholic church and of its undiminished hold upon the imaginations and loyalties of its adherents.

Are the cures genuine? I have no doubt but that many of them are. Certainly if faith and expectation, supported and sustained by the faith and prayers of a great company, can produce a healing effect, there is no likelier place for such a result.

The Catholic Church is both a religion and a form of government. To see its power and its weakness as a government, one should go to Rome. To realize its character as a religion, one should go to Lourdes.

RECENT RELAPSE TO MEDIAEVALISM

Catholicism is today less modern and more mediaeval in both doctrine and discipline than it was a generation ago. This may be an improvement—or it may not. There will be little attempt, in this chapter, to do more than state facts without passing judgments. And one of those facts is that the liberalizing movements within the church which were active thirty years ago have been either crushed out or driven under cover. This fact should be of equal interest to those who look upon the thirteenth century as the Golden Age and to those who believe either that the Catholic Church has imbibed something of the spirit of the twentieth century or that it ought to do so.

The term "Modernism" was first applied by its enemies, the Jesuits, to a type of Catholic thought which made use of the critical and historical methods which had become the common property of all scholars during the past century. It does not describe a particular body of results but a method of study and an attitude toward the problems which must arise in the minds of those who think seriously about religion. It is not based upon a philosophy which assumes that the supernatural is impossible, or upon practical objections to Catholic organization or papal infallibility.

It is merely a way of finding out the truth about the Bible, the history of the church, and the duties of Christians in the present age.

SCIENTIFIC METHOD IS BANNED

Although this method owes much to the work of non-Catholic German scholars—and that is one thing that puts the curse upon it—the first Catholics who conspicuously used it were a group of professors in the Institute Catholique at Paris. L. M. O. Duchesne wrote a book in which he exposed some of the fables of Catholic history. He had no hostility to these pious legends, but when he applied to them the ordinary tests of historical evidence as modern scholars have learned how to apply them, he found that they were without foundation. His book was put on the index of prohibited books in 1887. D'Hulst, the rector of the Institute, wrote a series of articles on Biblical subjects in which he used the methods of historical and literary criticism. There was nothing very radical in his conclusions, but, such as they were, they were the results of his own first-hand study of the documents. That was radicalism enough. The pope in 1893 issued the encyclical *"Providentissimus Deus"* condemning higher criticism and d'Hulst.

But the worst offender was Alfred Loisy, also a professor in the Institute Catholique. He wrote a history of the Old Testament canon, then one of the New Testament canon, and works on textual criticism and the synoptic problem. He was dismissed from his professorship. After remaining silent for a time, he published "The Gospel and the Church" in 1902. It was a reply to Harnack's "What Is Christianity?" but it employed some of the principles which Harnack had developed in his "History of Dogma." It was his opinion—and in this he was followed by other modernists—that the original and true gospel had become encrusted with doctrines which, whether true or not, were not a part of the message of Jesus and therefore not a part of the gospel. This was clearly at variance with the orthodox view that all the doctrines which the Catholic church has decreed from the second century to the nineteenth are but the explicit statement of truths which were implicit in the original "deposit of faith." Loisy's books were condemned by the Congregation of the Holy Office (the Inquisition) and also by the pope, and in 1908, after he had made outspoken comments upon certain decrees and encyclicals aimed against the modernists, he was excommunicated.

In Great Britain the chief exponent of modernism was George Tyrrell, an Irish priest who had become a convert to Roman Catholicism under the influence of Cardinal Newman. In his early books he had tried to reconcile strict Catholicism with the principle of development and a rational understanding of the universe. His "Letter to a Professor of Anthropology" was translated into Italian and published without his consent in January, 1906. It defended the Christian faith but by modernistic arguments. He was expelled from the Jesuit order, of which he had been a member for more than twenty years, and his reply to Pope Pius X's great encyclical of 1907 led to a condemnation which was the nearest thing possible to excommunication. When Cardinal Mercier in his "Modernism" attacked Tyrrell as a leading modernist, he replied with a book entitled "Mediaevalism." One of his favorite ideas was that the revelation of the will of God comes to men partly, at least, through their own experience.

In Italy the modernistic tendency found expression chiefly in studies in church history and in efforts toward social reform. Undoubtedly the pope did not exaggerate when he said that this influence was widespread among the clergy and in the seminaries. Prof. G. Luzzi, of Florence, is quoted as saying that, of any hundred clergy over forty years of age, sixty have the best products of modernistic literature in their private desks. Salvatore Minocchi edited a scholarly journal, *"Studi Religiosi"* at Florence from 1901 until 1907, when it was suppressed. Among his colleagues were Fracassini, rector of the seminary for priests at Perugia, and Gennochi, a professor in a seminary for priests at Rome. Father Bartoli, a brilliant and learned scholar who had been a Jesuit for twenty-seven years and a frequent contributor to *"Civiltà Cattolica,"* was commissioned to reply to an English attack on the primacy of Peter. His studies shook his faith in the historical basis for the church's claim and, after ten years of research, he joined the Waldensians.

Abbate Romolo Murri, who was never doctrinally
or even historically heretical, was a leader in that
aspect of modernism which relates to social reform and
in protesting against the attitude of the church as a
wealthy and powerful corporation indifferent to the
actual needs of the people. He was repeatedly disciplined between 1902 and 1907, and was then forbidden
to officiate as a priest. The novelist, Antonio Fogaz-
zaro, in 1906, published "The Saint," showing the
contrast between vital piety and the formal ecclesiastical program. The scene depicting the interview of
the "saint" with the pope was respectful toward the
pope as a man and as the head of Christendom, but
a flaming indictment of the conditions which made
him the head of a system which was too much concerned for its own power to care about the welfare
of souls. The book was placed on the Index, and
30,000 copies were sold in Italy the next month. It
had a wide circulation in English, French and German
translations.

THE WAR ON MODERNISM

What these modernists were trying to do was to
reform the church from the inside—the thing Luther
is criticized for not doing. Their basic principle was
that questions of scholarship should be settled by
scholarly investigations and not by the fiat of ecclesiastical authority. The reply to their arguments was a
series of edicts containing no argument whatever on
the merits of the questions but a reaffirmation of the

principle that these matters must be determined by authority. A summary of the most important of these pronouncements may be convenient, even if not very readable:

1879—Aug. 4, Leo XIII, encyclical *"Aeterni Patris,"* commanding study of Thomas Aquinas as the true Catholic philosophy.

1893—Nov. 18, encyclical *"Providentissimus Deus,"* against higher criticism.

1897—Jan. 13, decree of the Holy Office, approved by Leo XIII, prohibiting doubt as to the authenticity of the "three heavenly witnesses" passage (I John 7).

1899—September, letter to the French clergy upholding the traditional view of the Bible.

1902—October, Commission on Biblical studies established.

1904—January 23, encyclical enforcing Thomistic philosophy.

1906—June 27, Commission on Biblical Studies (enlarged so that critical scholars were in minority) decreed the Mosaic authorship of the Pentateuch.

July 28, Encyclical *"Pieni l'animo,"* to bishops of Italy, ordering exclusion of all modernists from seminaries and priesthood, forbidding young clerics from attending public universities and students in seminaries from reading newspapers and periodicals except one chosen by bishop.

1907—April 17, Piux X denounced modernistic heresies.

May 29, Commission on Biblical Studies decreed the Fourth Gospel to have been written by the Apostle John and to be strictly historical.

July 3, Holy Office, by decree *"Lamentabile sane,"* condemned 65 errors in Biblical inspiration and interpretation (the new syllabus of errors). The decree was signed by the pope.

September 8, Encyclical of Pius X, *"Pascendi."* The great anti-modernist encyclical.

November 18, confirmation of syllabus of July 3 and encyclical of September 8, and threat of excommunication for offenders.

November 21, *motu proprio* declaring all decrees of Commission on Biblical Studies binding on conscience.

December 16, pope thanks bishops for loyal support against modernism.

1910—September 1, *motu proprio* requiring anti-modernist oath.

It will be seen by a glance at this table that 1907 was the year of the great conflict over modernism. Before that time, modernists in the Roman Catholic Church were in danger. Since then, they have been outlaws.

The cardinal sin of the modernists is that they make too much of individual scholarship—that is, of reason—and too little of authority. They try to find out whether a certain verse in the first Epistle of John is part of the original text or an interpolation by studying the oldest existing manuscripts. They try to determine whether Moses wrote the Pentateuch and the Apostle John the gospel which bears his name by processes of literary and historical criticism, instead of accepting with docility the tradition of the church which says they did. This is the sin of pride. The great encyclical of Pius X thus describes them: "They disdain all authority and brook no restraint; and, relying upon a false conscience, they attempt to ascribe to a love of truth that which is in reality the result of pride and obstinacy." "With consummate audacity they criticize the church." No wonder Pius X was shocked. "Some of you," says Pius quoting Gregory IX, "puffed up like bladders with the spirit of vanity, strive by profane novelties to cross the boundaries fixed by the Fathers."

Even in the midst of this denunciation, the pope admits that the modernist scholars "lead a life of the greatest activity, of assiduous and ardent application to every branch of learning, and possess, as a rule, a reputation for irreproachable morality." This is generous of him, especially since only thirteen months before, in the *"Pieni l'animo"* encyclical, he had said: "Besides the most degrading corruption of morals, they have an open scorn for all authority and those who exercise it."

THE REAL ISSUE—NOT DOCTRINE BUT DISCIPLINE

But whatever may have been the personal virtues or vices of the modernists, upon which the pope varies his verdict according to the exigencies of his argument, he never wavers in his denunciation of them as resisters of the authority of the church. The issue was really a perfectly clear one, and from the point of view of the basic conception of the Roman Catholic church, the pope could not have done otherwise than to condemn those who put forward their own opinions upon matters of religious history, textual criticism, or Biblical interpretation, no matter how well fortified by their "assiduous application to every branch of learning," against the decisions of the constituted authorities.

For the pope sees, and very truly, that if scholarship has anything to do with finding the answers to these questions, then it will be impossible to prevent the laity from getting in an occasional word, for no one can pretend that ordination is an indispensable condition of scholarship. "We observe (in modernism) that most pernicious doctrine which would make of the laity the factor of progress in the church." Modernists think that the government and discipline of the church "must be brought into harmony with the modern conscience, which now wholly tends toward democracy; a share in ecclesiastical government should therefore be given to the lower ranks of the clergy, and even to the laity, and authority which is too much concentrated should be decentralized."

What then? Is there to be no progress in things religious? Certainly. But progress must be "according to the same dogma, the same sense, the same acceptation."

Because modernism is motived by "curiosity and pride," and because it is guilty of the basic error of putting individual opinion, even scholarly opinion, in place of ecclesiastical authority in the determination of historical and Biblical questions, it is "the synthesis of all heresies."

For a disease so serious, the treatment must be correspondingly drastic. Pius X makes his prescription as thorough as his diagnosis. He prescribes three medicines:

First, the scholastic philosophy, and especially the philosophy of Thomas Aquinas (died, 1274) must be made the basis of all the sacred sciences.

Second, bishops are ordered to "employ only in the lowest and obscurest offices" priests who show symptoms of modernism. They are to exclude from seminaries and Catholic universities "without compunction" any who are tainted with modernism, as well as any who extoll or excuse modernists or lend countenance to the movement "by carping at scholasticism and the Fathers and the magisterium of the church, or by refusing obedience to ecclesiastical authority in any of its depositories," and "those who show a love of novelty in history, archaeology or Biblical exegesis." "Far, far from the clergy be the love of novelty!" "Clerics and priests inscribed in a Catholic institute or university must not follow in the civil universities those courses for which there are chairs in the Catholic institutes to which they belong."

Third, prevent the writings of modernists from being read when published, and hinder their publication when they have not been. They are to be kept from university and seminary students more carefully than immoral books, because they are more dangerous. Catholic booksellers must not put on sale books condemned by the bishop, and even books that have received the *imprimatur* elsewhere must be scrutinized for fear they may have been approved through oversight.

In short, to revert to the words of the earlier encyclical, *"Pieni l'animo,"* of July 28, 1906, the way to exterminate this "growing band of rebels" is to "demand strictly from priests and clerics that *obedience* which, while absolutely obligatory upon all the faithful, constitutes for priests a principal part of their sacred duty," and to exclude absolutely "those who show inclinations . . . toward disobedience to discipline, and its parent, intellectual pride."

As for that aspect of modernism which leads its deluded devotees to promote "Christian action among the people" in the interest of social amelioration, this is not wrong in itself, but affords an excuse for independent activity and is therefore to be condemned. "In like manner in Catholic papers all such speech is to be condemned as . . . points toward 'new orientation of Christian life, new directions for the Church, new aspirations of the modern soul, a new social vocation for the clergy,' a new Christian civilization, and other like things."

The result has been as desired. Catholic modernism is dead. Some Catholics are more liberal than others, but to talk about a "liberal movement in the Catholic Church" is to talk of that which no longer exists.

FATHER HECKER AND "AMERICANISM"

Catholic "Americanism" is a technical term for a movement which came into existence shortly after the death of Father Hecker, the founder of the Paulist Fathers, in 1888, largely as a result of the discussion of his ideas, and which was brought to an abrupt end by a letter from Pope Leo XIII to Cardinal Gibbons on January 22, 1899.

Father Hecker was one of the most picturesque and one of the noblest characters that ever adorned the American priesthood. Born in 1819 of Lutheran parents, his first job was as an office boy with the Methodist paper, "Zion's Herald." After an extraordinary round of early experiences, including association with a radical "workingman's party," a stay

with the transcendental socialists at Brook Farm, and
a period of association with Bronson Alcott and
Orestes A. Brownson (then a socialist), he became a
convert to Catholicism and proposed to Thoreau that
they make a pilgrimage to Rome, begging their way
across Europe. The bishop approved, but Thoreau
declined. He united a deep piety and a determined
asceticism with an ardent social enthusiasm. He joined
the Redemptorist order and became a priest. Later
he was released from his Redemptorist vows, founded
the Paulist order and was made its superior. He was
indefatigable in holding missions for the conversion
of Protestants, in social service, and in writing and
publishing, was the founder of the "Catholic World"
and the Catholic Publication Society, and had raised
half of the funds necessary for the establishment of a
Catholic daily paper when ill health compelled him to
abandon that enterprise.

Father Hecker held that Catholicism alone was
consistent with the American love of liberty, but that
it must be a Catholicism imbued with a new spirit.
In a pamphlet published in 1875 he showed that
Catholic character had been weakened in the past by
too much emphasis upon obedience and by exaggerated emphasis upon the passive virtues. The new
age requires the cultivation of self-reliance and independent action. "The southern races, with their capacity for understanding the value of organization,
discipline, and the aesthetic aspects of religion, must
permit the northern races to satisfy their reason and

their inclination to an inner life within the church, even if the consequence should be a slighter observance of external forms." (Sedgwick in his brief biography.) The power of the Holy Spirit in each individual soul must be strengthened. This paper and others were republished in 1887 in "The Church and the Age."

This seems like the outline of a career of entire loyalty to the church, as indeed it was. Hecker believed in a strong church, even in papal infallibility, but he realized also the changed conditions of modern life. Men are needed, he said, "who will turn all the genuine aspirations of the age—in science, in socialism, in politics, in religion—which are now perverted against the church, into means of her defense and universal triumph."

After his death in 1888, discussion arose over his ideas. His biography by Elliott aroused controversy between the conservative party of no compromise and those Catholics who were more in sympathy with American institutions and modern ideas generally. There was a group of prelates who came to stand, in the public mind, for this more liberal attitude: Cardinal Gibbons, Archbishop Ireland, Archbishop Keane, rector of the Catholic University at Washington, Mgr. O'Connell, former rector of the American College at Rome, Mgr. O'Gorman, bishop of Sioux Falls, S. D., Archbishop Kain of St. Louis.

Archbishop Ireland wrote the preface to Elliott's Life of Hecker, calling him "the ideal American priest." In this preface Archbishop Ireland said: "It is as clear to me as noon-day light that countries and peoples have each their peculiar needs and aspirations as they have their peculiar environments, and that, if we would enter into souls and control them, we must deal with them according to their conditions. . . . Each century calls for its type of Christian perfection. At one time it was martyrdom; at another, the humility of the cloister. Today we need the Christian gentleman and the Christian citizen. An honest ballot and social decorum will do more for God's glory and the salvation of souls than midnight flagellations or Compostellan pilgrimages. . . . His (Hecker's) was the profound conviction that, in the present age, at any rate, the order of the day should be individual action—every man doing his full duty and waiting for no one else to prompt him. This, I take it, was largely the meaning of Father Hecker's oft-repeated teaching on the work of the Holy Ghost in souls."

Meanwhile, these liberal American prelates were fraternizing with their non-Catholic brethren more than any members of the Catholic hierarchy ever had before—or ever have since. Cardinal Gibbons opened the Chicago Parliament of Religions with prayer, in 1893. Archbishop Keane read papers before gatherings of Protestants, and gave an address before the International Scientific Congress of Catholics at Brussels, in 1894, expressing ideas very similar to Hecker's.

Mgr. O'Connell advocated these "American" ideas at the Catholic Scientific Congress at Freibourg in 1897.

Elliott's Life was translated into French with an admiring preface by Abbè Klein, a professor in the Institute Catholique in Paris—a dangerously modernistic place, as we have seen. Klein published an article on *"Le Catholicisme americain"* in 1897, repeating many of Hecker's ideas and some of his very phrases. He spoke of the progress in science, invention and intelligence in the past thirty years, and said that such material changes affect moral conditions and "demand more instruction, energy, independence, initiative, more aptitude to follow new discoveries and to renew methods and perhaps ideas." This means less respect for custom, which may now be a weakness and a hindrance instead of a virtue as heretofore, and the development of active rather than passive virtues.

THE DEATH-BLOW TO AMERICANISM

But a divergence of ideas soon developed. Abbè Maignan wrote a criticism of Hecker; the Archbishop of Paris refused to give it his *imprimatur*, but it was given by the Vatican. The Jesuits came into the fray. A. J. Delattre, S. J., wrote "Un Catholicisme americain" (1898) reprinting Klein's article with an answer to it which issued in the conclusion, "Christianity is docility." Leo XIII sent a letter to Mgr. Satolli, apostolic delegate to the United States, forbidding Catholics to take part in mixed congresses. This was a reproof for Cardinal Gibbons.

Then the pope wrote to Cardinal Gibbons, on Jan. 22, 1899, "Concerning New Opinions," and settled the whole matter: "It is known to you that the biography of Hecker . . . has excited not a little controversy . . . The underlying principle of these new opinions is that, in order more easily to attract those who differ from her, the church should shape her teachings more in accord with the spirit of the age and relax some of her ancient severity and make some concessions to new opinions . . . It does not need many words to prove the falsity of these ideas . . . But there is even a greater danger in that opinion of the lovers of novelty, according to which they hold that such liberty should be allowed in the Church that, her supervision and watchfulness being in some sense lessened, allowance be granted the faithful, each one to follow out more freely the leading of his own mind and the trend of his own proper activity. They are of opinion that such liberty has its counterpart in the newly given civil liberty which is now the right and the foundation of almost every secular state." The acceptance of the infallibility of the Pope is not enough, since some are contending "that the Holy Spirit pours richer and more abundant graces than formerly upon the souls of the faithful, so that without human intervention he teaches and guides them by some hidden instinct of his own." He objects to the views of those who undervalue the vows which religious orders take. (The Paulists had no vows.) "From the foregoing it is manifest that we are not able to give approval to those views which, in their collective sense, are called by some 'Americanism'."

Ireland, Keane and O'Connell denied that they had ever held the views which the pope condemned. Not another voice was ever raised in defense of them. "Americanism" was dead.

With the funeral of Americanism on Jan. 22, 1897, and of Catholic modernism on Sept. 8, 1907, ended all reasonable hopes on the one hand and fears on the other that the Roman Catholic Church either had allowed, or would in this generation allow, the modern spirit to have any influence upon its ideas, its attitudes, or its methods. Its last word is the word of the Jesuit Delattre, "Christianity is docility."

No more serious error can be made in judging of the spirit, the attitudes and the methods of Roman Catholicism in the United States at the present time than the assumption that it has been permeated and transformed in some subtle fashion by the spirit of American institutions. There would have been some justification for such an opinion thirty years ago. There is none now. That individual laymen exhibit modern attitudes, is of course true. But the attitudes of the hierarchy, the "teaching church," are unchangingly mediaeval, and the pressure of this hierarchy is exercised without cessation upon all faithful laymen— except when some specific object is to be attained by allowing the liberal utterance of a layman to go temporarily unrebuked.

XII

MORAL AND SOCIAL QUESTIONS

The chief stock in trade of the anti-Catholic books of a generation ago was vivid and venomous attacks upon the morals of the clergy and, to a less degree, of the laity. The general sense of mystery which surrounds the houses of the religious orders made it easy to represent them as dens of vice, and the secrecy of the confessional and the celibacy of the priesthood lent plausibility to the theory that the confession of sins was ordinarily the preliminary to more and worse sinning. Specifications and details were generally added, often in the form of "confessions" of ex-priests or ex-monks—sometimes perhaps true. It would be difficult to imagine that, where so much of opportunity is afforded, there are not some among the tens of thousands who go wrong. But that the priesthood and the religious orders are rotten with vice is a scandal unsupported by any evidence worthy of serious consideration. Stories of the debauchery of renaissance popes, of the corruption of the monasteries in the sixteenth century, and of priests who lived virtuously with one wife whom the church did not officially permit them to have but whom the community recognized as a lawful spouse, have no relevancy to the present situation. The theology of the Catholic church may not have become more liberal in recent centuries, but

244

the morals of its clergy have become more strict, and besides they probably never averaged as bad as they have been painted.

The Protestant impression of lax morality of the Catholic laity rests partly upon the fact that the Catholic church never excludes anyone for offenses against morality, and partly upon differences of custom due largely to differences of race and cultural tradition. The church does not cast members out of its fellowship for lapses from morality, because it has ways of dealing with them without doing so. There is the confessional; there is penance; there is the possibility of exclusion from the sacraments if the case is sufficiently serious. The theory is that it is better for a sinner to be within the church where he may still be exposed to the influences of grace and may sooner or later be brought to repentance, than for him to be cast out. However complacent the church may sometimes have seemed to be in regard to the existence of a "rough element" within it, no one who knows anything about it can say that the Catholic church is indifferent to morals and is satisfied with formal compliance with a routine of confession and penance without repentance and amendment of life. The existence of the Holy Name Society would by itself be a refutation of that charge.

CATHOLICS AND PROHIBITION

Catholics are, in general, on the wet side of the prohibition issue; this in spite of the Father Matthew

Temperance Society, and a strong organization of laymen favoring prohibition. Catholic papers are filled with attacks upon the prohibition law. The attitude, if not the argument, of a great part of the clergy is expressed by a letter from Bishop MacDonald (in "The Commonweal," March 28, 1928) who argues against prohibition on the grounds, first, that the Christian virtue of temperance cannot be exercised unless one is legally free to practice to the contrary, and, second, that Catholics must regulate their lives by Gospel standards and not by the edicts of "Caesar." Catholics should be sober "not because Caesar published an edict" but "because drunkards shall not possess the kingdom of God." "Total abstinence is nothing in God's eyes if the motive be not supernatural." Civil legislation in regard to alcohol is looked upon as an encroachment of "Caesar"—the United States government is always "Caesar" when it touches any subject even indirectly related to morals —upon the territory of either individual liberty or the control of the church. "Give Caesar an inch and he can be counted on to take an ell."

The Catholic championship of the cause of sex morality and "the Christian home" takes the form of opposition to divorce and birth-control. With regard to the latter topic, it is insistent upon the maintenance of the present federal law limiting the dissemination of information about contraceptive methods. In this case there seems to be neither apprehension about encroachments of Caesar upon the domain of moral legislation nor fear that compulsory ignorance of the methods of birth-control will deprive anyone of a free field in which to practice the Christian virtue of continence from "supernatural motives" alone. C. C. Martindale says ("Commonweal," Feb. 22, 1928): "I think that the frightful—I repeat, the frightful—burden rightly laid on the average Catholic citizen by way of the Catholic doctrine concerning birth restriction, tends to break down the allegiance of thousands whose shoulders are not exceptionally strong. I should not be in the least surprised to see, in a century, no Catholic country anywhere left, but strong, self-conscious, suffering Catholic minorities in every country."

MARRIAGE AND DIVORCE

The Catholic attitude in regard to marriage and divorce is determined by the doctrine that marriage is a sacrament. As such, the state can neither determine its conditions nor sever its bonds. Nor will the church itself either grant a divorce or (save in certain exceptional cases) a nullification of a marriage. If its policy stopped here, the consistency and good faith of its position would be unassailable. But the practice of the church in granting declarations of nullity *ab initio* for any one of more than fifty reasons exposes it to grave charges of inconsistency and worse. Two or three recent cases have exhibited all the weaknesses of this system.

In one of these, which attained wide publicity owing to the social prominence of the parties—a daughter of one of America's richest families and an English duke—the supposedly married pair lived together for twenty-five years, and the ostensible wife bore two sons to the man whom two officiating bishops, the laws of the state and public opinion declared to be her husband. At the end of that quarter-century of apparently married life, during which she had accepted and enjoyed, or endured, the status of wife, the lady secured a divorce. Both parties entered into new marriages. Then the duke contemplated entering the Catholic church. But since that church does not recognize the validity of any divorce, the status of the duke appeared to be that of a man who was "living in sin" with a woman who was not his wife, since the second marriage could not be valid if the first one was. Upon application to the Rota, the court at Rome having jurisdiction over marriage causes, he secured a judgment that his first marriage was no marriage at all. The difficulty was thus cleared away and he was eligible for admission to the Catholic church.

The ground for the declaration of nullity was that the bride had not acted under her own free will. It is not alleged that physical violence or actual coercion had been employed, but there was such insistent appeal and pressure by her mother that her resistance was finally broken down. Apparently there was no more compulsion than was involved in making it so unpleasant for the poor girl to refuse her titled suitor that she finally decided to accept him to escape her mother's nagging. It is not asserted that the family

had a follow-up system so effective as to compel her
to remain with her supposed husband against her will.
Nor is it denied that for twenty-five years she accepted whatever advantages there may have been in
the status of duchess and became, if not his wife by
virtue of the ceremony and the laws of the state and
the blessing of two bishops, then his common-law wife
without benefit of clergy. There is probably not another court in Christendom, even in Nevada, France,
Mexico, or Moscow, or wherever else the "divorce
evil" is supposed to be most rampant, where a case
so frivolous would have gotten a favorable hearing.
It is explained that the children of the marriage which
was declared never to have existed are legitimate children, born in wedlock, because the declaration of nullity affects nothing except the relation of the parties
to the Catholic church. They were married enough
to have legitimate children but not married enough
to interfere with a subsequent marriage with the blessing of the church. All this reduces to nothing better
than a disreputable ecclesiastico-legal fiction by which
the church agrees to pretend that, for the specific and
sole purpose of rendering an individual eligible for
membership, his ostensible marriage was no marriage
at all, while for every other purpose it was entirely
valid.

A PAPAL CHAMBERLAIN ADVERTIZES

And all of this in the interest of maintaining a
professedly higher standard of domestic morality and

a level of social purity to which the state and the
Protestants do not attain! Nothing could be much
more demoralizing to ethical standards in reference to
domestic ties than to set up a confusion in which no
person who respects the decisions of the papal courts
can be quite sure whether he is married or not or, if
so, to what extent and in what relations. For it must
be remembered that the decision of the court does not
profess to have undone anything. It merely declares
that something was never done which everybody supposed had been done. There must be ten thousand
couples now living together in the bonds of more or
less holy wedlock who have reason to suspect that the
consent of one member was obtained only after the
exercise of considerable pressure from relatives and
friends. They can never know whether they are really
married or not until the Rota, or a diocesan court,
passes upon their cases.

In that connection it is interesting to recall the
report (in "The Living Church, Nov. 5, 1927) that
a certain "papal chamberlain, attorney and counselor
at canon law, from Rome," has been circulating his
business card bearing a New York address announcing
that he "has opened an office at the above address for
the purpose of dealing with the annulment of marriages in the Roman Catholic church and all matters
pertaining to canon law. Advice Free." Catholic
editors, who were invited to express an opinion of
this effort of a "papal chamberlain" to work up business in the annulment of marriages, expressed no in-

dignation except against the paper which had given publicity to the matter. A priest defended the "papal chamberlain." "Any marriage that is annullable is, in the eyes of the Roman Catholic church, no marriage at all. To put people into a position where they can receive the sacraments and live in a state of grace is not a dishonorable motive." Which confirms the suggestion that there must be many parties to "annullable marriages" who do not know whether they are married or not—especially since annulments can be had on such flimsy pretexts.

Nevertheless it should be said that, in spite of these devious methods of preventing the permanence of marriage from being an intolerable burden or an insuperable obstacle to the admission of divorced persons to the church, the stand of the Roman Catholic church in regard to marriage has value in opposing reckless and ill considered divorce.

ACTION FOR SOCIAL WELFARE

The attitude of the church on those great questions of social justice and human welfare growing out of the tensions of the economic process has varied too widely to be fairly characterized in a sentence. Its constituency in the United States has contained a larger percentage of the poor and the laboring classes than any Protestant church. The high point in official Catholic approval of modern labor legislation and the application of humanitarian principles and Christian

ethics to the industrial situation was the encyclical of
Leo XIII, *"Rerum Novarum,"* 1891. In this he challenged the doctrine of *laissez faire* and reliance upon
purely economic forces to regulate the relations between capital and labor, and urged that "the first concern of all is to save the poor workers from the cruelty
of greedy speculators who use human beings as mere
instruments for money-making." He overcame the
habitual Catholic aversion to governmental action in
a field that is certainly not unrelated to that of morals,
to the extent of advocating legislation for the limitation of hours of labor, for the reduction of occupa-
tional hazards, and for the special protection of women
and children in industry. He defended the principle
of labor unions and collective bargaining both by practical considerations and by quoting his favorite St.
Thomas Aquinas. It was this encyclical which earned
for Leo XIII the designation of "the workingman's
pope."

It was not a recantation of these sentiments, but
rather a reflection of the Italian political situation
and especially a renewed protest against the alleged
"spoliation" of the papacy, when, after the pope had
commanded Italian Catholics to abstain from participation in political life so long as the papacy remained
in its "painful, precarious and intolerable position"
(1898), the Sacred Congregation of Extraordinary
Ecclesiastical Affairs in 1902 directed the popular
Christian movement to abandon its advocacy of such
"novelties" as the restriction of child-labor, an eight-

hour law, old-age pensions, and the encouragement of the use of Sunday as a rest day, and focus its attention upon the restoration of the temporal sovereignty of the pope. It was also significant that these social reforms were being advocated chiefly by those who showed symptoms of "modernism." In fact, it was one of the signs of their modernism that they were promoting these causes without the sanction of their bishops, who were much more interested in other things.

The most potent Catholic organization in the United States for the promotion of social reforms as well as the interests of the church is the National Catholic Welfare Council. Its six departments—education, press and publicity, laws and legislation, executive, social action, and lay organizations, with their ramifying bureaus and committees—foster every form of Catholic action. In this connection the bureaux of industrial relations, of social welfare, of rural problems, of motion pictures, of immigration, and of training for welfare work are the most important. The N. C. W. C. has had the advantage of expert leadership in these departments, including such men as Mr. John A. Lapp, who was president of the National Conference of Social Work in 1927, and whose recent book, "Justice First" (The Century Co., 1928), is as fine a statement of a truly liberal and comprehensive policy of governmental action for social welfare as one could hope to find.

CATHOLIC CHARITY

This scientific approach to problems of social welfare is a new thing in Catholic circles, but Catholic charity is a very old thing. Many of the religious orders have for centuries been exclusively devoted to work for the poor, and the more than a thousand orphanages, hospitals and homes for the aged in the United States alone testify to a practical interest in the unfortunate. These institutions are partly sustained by grants of public money, and their utility for purposes of propaganda is considerable. The nursing sisters are given specific instruction in the art of presenting Catholicism to the favorable consideration of their patients.

It is possible, however, that Roman Catholics take to themselves too much credit for a superior quality of Christian charity as they do for the exclusive possession of religious truth. A Catholic editor, for example, thinks that it is a deadly defect of Protestant charity that it regards destitution merely as a public nuisance to be abated by whatever means may be most efficacious, and that "by consecrating wealth as a symbol of merit, it abandoned this old (Catholic) attitude of reverence for the deprived folk who, in a homely phrase full of significance, were once termed 'God's poor'." No doubt an undue reverence for wealth has characterized the culture of Protestant countries, as an undue reverence for rank has characterized Catholic countries, though the proof that the former attitude is the result of Protestant principles, and specifically of Calvinism, seems less convincing than it did when the theory was first suggested.

But there are not merely two possible attitudes towards poverty. There are three. Poverty may be considered as a public nuisance to be abated in the interest of the prosperous. This develops a heartless institutionalism. It is clearly inadequate and un-Christian. Or the poor may be "God's poor," to be the objects of perpetual charity as well as sympathy, on the theory that God is perfectly satisfied to have his poor remain poor. "They are farther from the sun but, for their very suffering, appreciably nearer heaven." This has commonly been the presupposition of Catholic charity. But the idea that poverty is the gift of God and a means of grace, except in isolated cases, involves a still more odious consecration of the status quo. It is the prosperous who complacently recommend to all men to live content in that state in which it has pleased God to call them. But it becomes clear, as the causes of poverty are studied, that modern poverty does not result from the calling of a definite group to a life of destitution for their soul's welfare and to provide for those of more fortunate estate a field for the exercise of Christian charity, but rather from human greed and ignorance and from the fact that we have not yet learned how to operate successfully the industrial machinery which we have constructed. Poverty is a social disease to be cured by the medicine of social justice. We shall always need the good Samaritans to pick up those who fall by the wayside, but we ought also to let some of our altruism take the constructive form of cleaning out the robbers that infest the road.

It is from this point of view that the very title of Lapp's book is indicative of a new spirit in Catholic charities—"Justice First."

XIII

CATHOLIC POETRY AND THE CATHOLIC MIND

Cardinal Newman's great hymn, "Lead, Kindly Light," has sometimes been cited as the most perfect of all Catholic poems, expressing beautifully the soul's escape from the disastrous pride of individualism and the peace of surrender to the church. It would be that, except for one circumstance. Consider it, with annotations and foot-notes suggesting what might be imagined to be the meanings intended by a cardinal who was a convert from Protestantism:

Lead, kindly Light,[1] amid the encircling gloom.
    Lead thou me on.
The night is dark[2] and I am far from home.
    Lead thou me on.
Keep thou my feet[3]; I do not ask to see
The distant scene. One step enough for me.

I was not ever thus,[4] nor prayed that thou
    Shouldst lead me on;
I loved to choose and see my path,[5] but now
    Lead thou me on.
I loved the garish day,[6] and spite of fears[7]
Pride ruled my will.[8] Remember not past years.[9]

[1]The church. [2]Darkness of mere reason. [3]Submission to the church. [4]When I was a Protestant. [5]False liberty as a Protestant. [6]Of reason. [7]The doubts which reason only raises and cannot lay. [8]Pride of opinion, the typical Protestant vice, vs. submission to authority. [9]Now that I have made my submission to the church.

The one circumstance which interferes with this interpretation is that the hymn was written in 1833. Newman did not become a Catholic until 1845. This great "Catholic" hymn was written by Newman while he was still a Protestant.

Catholicism lends itself with peculiar readiness to poetic statement, as will easily be seen by anyone who will consult any of the recent anthologies of Catholic verse: "An Anthology of Catholic Poets," compiled by Shane Leslie (Macmillan, 1926), "The Book of Modern Catholic Verse," compiled by Theodore Maynard (Holt, 1926), and "The Catholic Anthology," edited by Thomas Walsh (Macmillan, 1927).

Catholic anthologists commonly make little or no distinction between Catholic poetry and poetry by Catholic writers. There is, however, a difference. A Catholic golfer does not play Catholic golf. A Catholic mathematician does not teach Catholic mathematics. A Catholic poet may or may not write Catholic poetry. They naturally include the pre-Protestant poets, such as Chaucer. Leslie's criterion of a Catholic poet is one who died in the faith, even if all his poetry was written before his submission to the church. This takes in Dryden, Pope, Wycherley, Rossetti, and even one so little Catholic as Oscar Wilde.

A classification of 235 poems included in Leslie's collection shows 59 distinctively Catholic, 31 religious but not distinctively Catholic, 13 dealing with morality but not specifically Catholic, 132 miscellaneous secular poems only incidentally, if at all, Catholic or even religious. Of the 59 distinctly Catholic religious poems, 3 treat of Catholic forms of worship, 3 give a Catholic view of Christ or narrate legends about him, 8 reflect Catholic morality or philosophy of life, 11 are in honor of the church or the clergy, 13 are in praise of the saints or tell legends about them, 21 are devoted to the exaltation of the Virgin Mary.

Readers who have skipped the figures in the above paragraph as dull statistics, would do well to go back and read them with some care. They help to answer the question, why Catholicism lends itself to poetic treatment. It is worth noting that, so far as distinctively Catholic poetry is concerned, the most popular themes are the Virgin Mary, the saints, and the church.

Catholic writers make rather extravagant claims with reference to the influence of their religion upon poetry. Maynard, in the introduction to his anthology, says: "Protestantism has not, with one remarkable exception, produced poets. And the reason is that Protestantism is a negative thing spiritually and is positive only as a method of political and social organization. When a poet of our civilization prays, his face at once turns towards Rome." (The exception, of course, is Milton.) Thus Spenser, Wordsworth, Coleridge, Edgar Lee Masters and Vachel Lindsay—much as it would surprise the last two, at least —are said to have shown their "Catholic hearts," and "even Milton cannot wholly be claimed by Protestantism" because his verse is full of that "pomp and gold" which his puritanism led him to repudiate as a factor in religion.

The truth rather is that when a poet prays, or when a pray-er poetizes, he casts his thought into an imaginative rather than a didactic mold, and seeks imagery wherever he can find it regardless of its doctrinal or ecclesiastical implications.

Catholicism lends itself to poetic expression because it is emotional and uncritical. Fostering an attitude of credulity, it can utilize an accumulated store of imaginative and legendary material in good faith. Making more of a mystical contemplation of the sufferings of Christ than of his ethical teachings, its poets dwell with vivid realism and imaginative sympathy upon the details of his passion. Early examples of this are in the eighth century "Dream of the Rood," and the anonymous lines on the Holy Cross ending,

> "Sweet be the nails
> And sweet the tree,
>   And sweeter the burden that hangs upon thee."

But these are neither better poetry nor better mysticism than the lines of the Protestant, Sidney Lanier,

> "Into the wood my Master went—"

The rich personnel of saints and heroes of the faith which Catholicism honors furnishes a numerous and varied *dramatis personae*, sufficiently remote in time and place to have romantic appeal quite apart from whatever religious values they may embody but affording also a concrete and pictorial embodiment of religious aspiration. The legends of the saints are readily susceptible of poetic expression, and the vivid sense of an encompassing cloud of witnesses and a marching host of companions of Christ has both an aesthetic and a spiritual value. Lionel Johnson sees this army of the Lord thus in their gallant array:

Ah, see the fair chivalry come, the companions of Christ,
  White horsemen, who ride on white horses, the Knights
    of God!
They for their Lord and Lover who sacrificed
  All, save the sweetness of treading where he first trod!

Now, whithersoever he goeth, with him they go;
  White horsemen, who ride on white horses, oh fair to see!
They ride where the rivers of Paradise flash and flow,
  White horsemen, with Christ their Captain, forever He!

But there are those who would claim that the consciousness of the communion of saints is no exclusive possession of those who accept their legends as historical, venerate them as intercessors, and preserve their bones in reliquaries as means of cultivating their favor.

The adoration of the Virgin Mary makes possible a spiritualized version of love for a lady and loyalty to a queen—two themes which lend themselves with peculiar facility to poetic uses. She is the "Queen of Courtesy." In a bold figure she appeals to man to "leave thy sin then for my sake" and "take me for thy wife," in a fourteenth century poem. She is the "Queen of Heaven, of Hell eke Emperess, Lady of this world," in the lines of the fifteenth century priest, John Lydgate. She is the "Star of the Sea, man's Mediatrice to God omnipotent," with the sixteenth century priest, Alexander Barclay. She is the perfect mother as well as the perfect queen and the fairest lady. She is the mystic rose growing in the gardens of God. Frederick William Faber sums up in this sonnet the salutary graces and the saving love of Mary in a turbulent world:

I looked upon the earth; it was a floor
For noisy pageant and rude bravery—
Wassail and arms and chase among the high,
And burning hearts uncheered among the poor;
And gentleness from every land withdrew.
Methought that beds of whitest lilies grew
All suddenly upon the earth in bowers;
And gentleness, that wandered like a wind,
And nowhere could meet sanctuary find,
Passed like a dewey breath into the flowers.
Earth heeded not; she still was tributary
To kings and knights, and man's heart well-nigh failed;
Then were the natural charities exhaled
Afresh, from out the blessed love of Mary.

Poetry expressive of the Catholic philosophy of life and principles of conduct are by no means all ascetic. Most of them lean rather in the opposite direction, for asceticism is a specialized virtue reserved to those who have a special gift or calling for it. To be sure, there is Gerard Hopkins' praise of the "Habit of Perfection," with its exaltation of silence, fasting and poverty. But there are also old Lenten rhymes expounding the best methods for alleviating the rigors of the Lenten limitations upon diet and hinting that it is the devil's business that "of all the days in the week he makes Friday."

Mr. Maynard, in the introduction to his admirable "Book of Modern Catholic Verse," is clearly proud of the fact that, while "it is impossible to imagine a Protestant writing a religious drinking song," "Mr. Chesterton is nowhere in his writings more Catholic than in his drinking songs." "God and not the devil presides over the festive board where Catholics sit," says Mr. Maynard. "For this reason Mr. Belloc wrote his superb 'Drinking Song of the Pelagian Heresy,' uttering as he did so, as a learned Jesuit said to me, a condemnation even stronger than that of St. Germanus." And since this rollicking and euphonious song is taken seriously by learned authorities as a true reflection of the Catholic philosophy of life—as I agree that it is—it may be well to close with a portion of that admirable lyric. Pelagius, it is to be understood, had announced a doctrine which made the salvation of man depend rather upon his own decisions than upon the church.

> Whereat the Bishop of old Auxerre—
>   Germanus was his name—
> He tore great handfuls out of his hair,
>   And he called Pelagius shame.
> And then with his stout episcopal staff
>   So thoroughly thwacked and banged
> The heretics all, both short and tall,
>   That they rather had been hanged.

Semi-Chorus

Oh, he thwacked them hard and he thwacked
*   them long*
*   On each and all occasions,*
Till they bellowed in chorus loud and strong
*   Their orthodox persuasions.*

Chorus

With my row-ti-dow-ti-oodely-ow,
*   Their orthodox persuasions.*

Now the Faith is old and the Devil bold—
    Exceedingly bold indeed;
And the masses of doubt that are floating about
    Would smother a mortal creed.
But we who sit in a sturdy youth
    And still can drink strong ale—
Let us put it away to infallible truth
    That always shall prevail.

Semi-Chorus

So thank the Lord for the temporal sword,
*   And for howling heretics, too,*
And for all the good things that our Christendom
*   brings—*
*   But especially barley brew!*

Chorus

With my row-ti-dow-ti-oodely-ow,
*   Especially barley brew!*

This was not put forth as a complete exposition
of Catholic theology and morals, and it is not here
presented as such. Still, it has its merits as covering

the field in bare but suggestive outline. *First,* "infallible truth that always shall prevail." *Second,* "the temporal sword" as the means of making it prevail—not here and now, of course, but when and where the conditions are favorable for the exercise of that instrument of grace and persuasion—and the "howling heretics" as the visible and vocal symbol of its triumph. *Third,* "especially barley brew," as the token of the non-ascetic Christian man's rightful enjoyment of the good things of life, his freedom from Puritan prejudices and limitations, and his personal liberty in all that is not of faith or morals.

Because of "barley brew" and the principle for which it stands—the principle of non-interference with the conduct of the individual in matters which the church has not included in the field of its control of morals—the Catholic church allows to its members more latitude in habits and customs than most Protestant communions and, in particular, refuses to use its influences in favor of such policies as prohibition and strict Sunday observance.

Because of the "temporal sword" principle, the Catholic church has in times past both wielded a civil power of its own and brought pressure to bear on civil governments for the extirpation of heresy, the enforcement of its own teaching and discipline, and its establishment in a preferred position in the state. Catholics living under liberal governments in non-Catholic states, such as the United States, sincerely assert that no such policy enters into the program of the church under these conditions, but no authorized spokesman for the church has ever repudiated the often repeated claim that the church has a right to adopt such a policy whenever in its judgment the conditions seem favorable to its successful application.

Because of its claim to possess "infallible truth that always shall prevail," it will be dominant where it can and patient where it must, but it can neither compromise nor parley with those who do not accept its claims. Christ has "ordered the whole of mankind to believe the truths expounded to them by witnesses chosen by God"—as the pope says in his encyclical of Jan. 6, 1928—that is, by the Roman hierarchy and, as the final arbiter, by the pope himself. Therefore the church must reject the overtures of those who would "treat with the Roman church upon the basis of equality of rights and as equals." Coming just at the time when American Catholics are seeking to "participate more openly, fruitfully and industriously in the nation's political, moral, social and creative business" (G. N. Shuster: "The Catholic Spirit in America," New York, 1927, p. x), this encyclical reveals no new attitude on the part of that church, but it clarifies the situation and discloses its difficulties.

Between the Catholic church and other churches there can be no fellowship, because the former will have no fellowship except submission. Between individual Catholics and non-Catholics there must be cooperation in social, industrial and political life. Living side by side, they cannot be strangers and it is better that they should be friends than enemies. Liberal-minded non-Catholics will enter heartily into such cooperation, insisting only that it shall be such as will not tend to put into the hands of the church the control, which it claims as its right, over an area in which the American state asserts its jurisdiction, or to give to the Catholic church the pre-eminence and predominance to which it has never ceased to lay claim.

Date Due